the Game of Singles in Tennis

By the same authors:

the Game of Doubles in Tennis

the Game of Singles in Tennis

by William F. Talbert and Bruce S. Old

Drawings by Ed Vebell and Katharine D. Old

Diagrams by Stephen P. Baldwin

J. B. LIPPINCOTT COMPANY • *PHILADELPHIA and NEW YORK*

Drawings on pages 16, 36, 44, 145 adapted by Katharine D. Old from photographs courtesy of Max Peter Haas.

Drawings on pages 22, 50, 70, 106, 109, 144 adapted by Katharine D. Old from photographs courtesy of World Tennis *magazine.*

Drawing on page 18 adapted by Katharine D. Old from photograph following page 177, Match Play and the Spin of the Ball *by William T. Tilden and drawing on page 111 adapted by Katharine D. Old from photograph Plate XI,* The Art of Lawn Tennis *by William T. Tilden, both published by Methuen, London, 1928 and 1920.*

Drawing on page 75 adapted by Katharine D. Old from photograph page 78 by Arthur E. Haug, How to Win at Tennis *by John A. Kramer, Ziff-Davis Publishing Co., Chicago, 1949.*

Drawings, by Ed Vebell, on pages 34, 46–49, 104, 105, 134–142 and some of the text and captions on these pages have appeared in somewhat different form in Sports Illustrated *magazine and in* Sports Illustrated Book of Tennis, *J. B. Lippincott Company, Philadelphia and New York, copyright © 1958, 1959, 1960 by TIME Inc.*

The diagrams on pages 39, 41, 61, 82, 100 and 122 and some of the accompanying text in somewhat different form have appeared in Sports Illustrated *magazine, copyright © 1962 by TIME Inc.*

ISBN-0-397-00212-2

Eleventh Printing

PRINTED IN THE UNITED STATES OF AMERICA

LIBRARY OF CONGRESS CATALOG CARD NUMBER 62-14232

foreword

The aspiring tennis player has long been in need of a complete and authoritative analysis of the game of singles—a book he can study in order to improve his tactics as well as his stroke production. In our opinion, Bill Talbert and Bruce Old have combined their knowledge to fill this void. And we feel they have been just as successful for singles with *The Game of Singles in Tennis* as they were previously for doubles with their "bible" entitled *The Game of Doubles in Tennis*.

This book contains just the right amount of historical information on the development of tennis to whet the appetite and set the stage for a searching study of the modern game of singles. The excellent chapters on the stroke production methods and tactics of the serve, return of service, net play and base line play are made all the more valuable by detailed analyses of how tennis matches are won. In addition, there are numerous instructive diagrams of actual points taken from tournament play. Finally, there is a summary chapter which provides an excellent review for ready reference.

We know of the soundness of the teachings of Bill Talbert from his long and devoted service to tennis as a player, as a Captain of the U. S. Davis Cup Team and as a developer of many young players. We welcome this expert presentation of the game of singles. It is particularly timely in view of the new emphasis on physical fitness stemming from the White House. We commend this book to all tennis players—beginners and experts, young and old.

Don Budge

Jack Kramer

contents

introduction

The purpose of this book is to attempt to present in a detailed yet readable manner the basic fundamentals of the game of singles in tennis. While there have been a number of books written dealing with stroke production and with certain phases of singles play, no truly comprehensive presentation of the many facets of this great game has ever been published.

The authors believe that most players, whether they are of the tournament circuit variety, or occasional weekend enthusiasts, or merely beginners, can profit to a marked degree by a study of the game. In this way the player can develop his game so that he will habitually try the proper shots at the correct moment and thus utilize his own particular talents to maximum advantage. Naturally, the talents and the style of each player vary, so that we have attempted to cover the subject in a manner which will be helpful to all types of players.

To assist the reader, a number of drawings and diagrams have been included to illustrate clearly the methods of stroke production, and the positions of the players and movement of the ball in complete singles points taken from actual matches. A typical example of the latter is given in figure 1 in order to present the method and symbols utilized.

While it may seem like wishing for the stars, it is our hope that this book will assist in some small way the development of singles play in the United States, to the end that we will regain our former enviable position as the producer of the best players in this great international game.

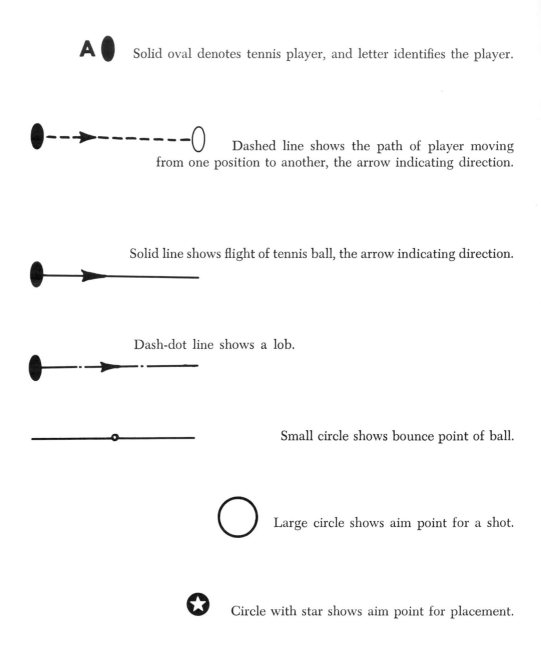

A ● Solid oval denotes tennis player, and letter identifies the player.

Dashed line shows the path of player moving from one position to another, the arrow indicating direction.

Solid line shows flight of tennis ball, the arrow indicating direction.

Dash-dot line shows a lob.

Small circle shows bounce point of ball.

Large circle shows aim point for a shot.

Circle with star shows aim point for placement.

Diagram Method

This figure illustrates the method used to diagram points in this book. It also serves to show how two mistakes by player A cost him this particular point.

Player A serves deep to the backhand of player B and then rushes the net to volley the return. Receiver B hits a cross-court backhand return of service which server A volleys back, but, in doing so, makes his first mistake by not hitting it sufficiently deep. This gives receiver B, who had retreated to the defensive base line position, an opportunity to move forward and take the offense. Server A then makes his second and final mistake. He starts moving very rapidly to his right to cover a possible cross-court return. While this move is in the proper direction, player A has made the common, fatal mistake of overcommitting himself by running too far cross court. In his haste he continues to move and he is not in a balanced position from which he could have a chance of covering the backhand as well as the forehand side. As player B moves forward he notes this situation carefully and decides to place his passing shot down the line behind the moving netman. As shown, this brings well-deserved success.

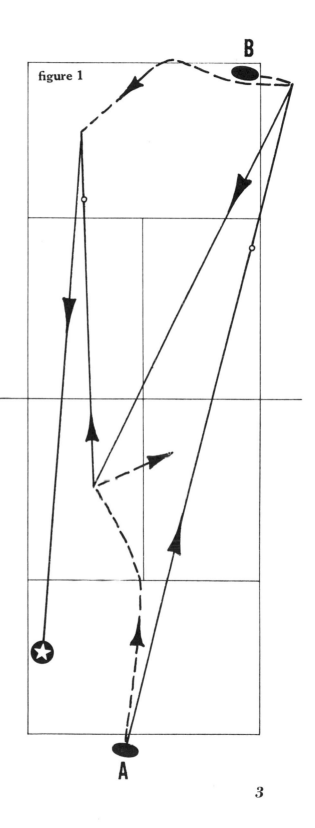

figure 1

the
Greatest
of
Individual
Sports

There is really little or no doubt about it—the game of singles in tennis represents the ultimate in individual international sports.

Since we wish to avoid at all cost alienating at the outset any readers who are golf, swimming, boxing, track, bowling, billiards, squash, fencing, wrestling, etc. enthusiasts, let us immediately consider the justification for this claim. Those who need convincing should ponder the following:

It is international.

Tennis is the most international of all sports. Singles is played the world over by both sexes, young and old. It is played in big cities and small towns, at exclusive clubs and public playgrounds, indoors and outdoors, by people from all walks of life. The smooth, rhythmic, intensely athletic nature of the game provides absorbing interest not only to the contestants, but also to the gallery, making it a top spectator sport everywhere. Some forty nations compete each year for the renowned Davis Cup, symbol of the world's championship among the nations. It is not unusual to have representatives from twenty nations competing for the famous Wimbledon and United States singles titles.

It requires skill and speed.

Tennis is a game which goes true to form. To play through a best of five sets singles match leaves little chance for doubt as to the more skillful player—luck has essentially no bearing when the ball will have to be hit over the net some one thousand times in a match! Stroke production, style, speed, footwork, timing, tactics and accuracy cannot but assert themselves over this extended period of chasing and stroking a

5

ball which sometimes travels at speeds around 100 miles per hour. And, to further accentuate the requirements for skill, the ball often takes erratic bounces, forcing changes of plans to be calculated with phenomenal rapidity. Tennis is truly a game of tenths of seconds and tenths of inches played at breakneck speed.

It requires generalship.

The great Anthony Wilding once said: "Perfect style, inexhaustible stamina, even the best strokes are of no avail if the brain that governs the hand is not taking stock of strategical positions and planning moves by which winning coups may be achieved." Ingenious strategy and tactics give infinite variety to the game and bring about the possibility of upsets. When players possess nearly equal stroke capability, the match is won by the man utilizing the superior generalship. He is the player who studies the style, strokes and psychology of his opponent in order to learn his strengths and weaknesses and anticipate his moves. With this knowledge he can feed the shots, spin, change of pace, depth and angles, and utilize the position play needed to upset the opponent's game and thus win the match. He can also sense just that moment when the tide of the battle is turning, when a change in tactics is required, and how to seize and exploit every opportunity. To accomplish this requires tremendous and undivided powers of concentration. Tennis is certainly the most intellectual of active sports.

It requires stamina.

William T. Tilden once said: "Tennis puts an athlete under the hardest physical, mental and nervous strain of any game played by mankind." Unequivocal backing for this statement has come from numerous two- and three-sport athletes. It was concurred in, for example, by Joe Hunt, who played varsity football, and by Tony Trabert, who played varsity basketball, when each was at the top of U. S. tennis. Tennis requires stamina not only because of the great amount of running, quick starts, stops and changes of direction over a two- to three-hour period, but also because the generalship one must exercise places on the system a mental and a nervous strain which serves to compound severely the fatigue problems. Think of the total number of decisions involving complex factors of stroke production and tactics which a tennis player must make within a half-second time allowance during the course of a five-set match! No wonder tennis players are completely exhausted after a tough encounter and find it difficult to be at top form all the way through a tournament.

It requires courage.

One of the qualities which stands out in great tennis players, whether club or world champions, is an unquenchable spirit of courage. It is exemplified by the will to win and the determination to overcome all odds. Could anyone ever watch a match played by a William M. Johnston, a Bitsy Grant or a Ted Schroeder without having indelibly imprinted on his mind a vision of sheer courage? Just when all seems lost and a tennis player is too tired to think, or to toss the ball up for the next serve, he must be able to reach down for his last ounce of reserve strength and fight his way back. There is no other way to explain such comebacks as the famous Davis Cup victory of Don Budge over Baron Gottfried Von Cramm after being down 1-4 in the fifth set. The great Norman Brookes and Henri Cochet were at their best just when they seemed hopelessly beaten. They were as cool under fire as the proverbial iceberg. And do you know the story of the 1921 Davis Cup match when Tilden played despite a dangerously infected foot? He promptly lost the first two sets and was within two points of defeat before winning the third set 7-5 from the Japanese star, Zenzo Shimizu. Although every step was painful, and the physican who lanced the infection during the rest period advised his default, Tilden refused to quit. He held on grimly and finally won in five sets. History is replete with such incidents of courage on the tennis court.

It has a tradition of sportsmanship.

Singles breeds sportsmanship. When playing without an umpire, each player must call all balls on his side of the net. It is an unwritten rule that one always gives his opponent the benefit of the doubt on close decisions. During a club match it is rare that you fail to find a receiver calling a shot good, only to have the striker refuse to accept the call because he believed the ball was out. Perhaps the most celebrated incident of this type occurred in a Davis Cup match. J. C. Parke of England hit an overhead smash away for game, set and Davis Cup match against Norman E. Brookes of Australia. However, Parke walked over to the umpire and informed him that his racket touched the net on his follow-through. After some discussion the umpire awarded the point to Brookes, who proceeded to take advantage of this life-giving break to lift his game and win the match, ultimately giving Australia the Davis Cup.

The tradition of the game also calls for courtesy, a minimum of temperament display and no alibis. The previously mentioned incident concerning Tilden's infected foot was never revealed by Tilden himself. It came to light only after his death through the writings of Vincent Richards, who was present in the dressing room during the rest period visit of the physician.

It is available to all.

The existence of tennis courts all over the world, coupled with the inexpensive nature of tennis equipment permits all people to play singles. The fact that one can transport his equipment easily, and is able to get plenty of exercise in one hour, adds much to the appeal of the game. And you do not have to collect a team—you need only two people to play.

Now combine these multiple attributes of broad international competition, skill, speed, generalship, stamina, courage, sportsmanship and easy availability to all, and you have in the game of singles in tennis the greatest of individual sports. How can anyone think otherwise as he contemplates the pleasures and intricacies of the game?

Every reader must understand that singles is a game in which he might excel, because its infinite variety makes for champions of remarkable diversity of style and physique. Be you beginner, weekend player or champion you can inspire yourself to greater heights by sitting back in your easy chair, closing your eyes and visualizing the following historical parade: the smooth, sporting, perfection of the Dohertys, the tactical guile of the ageless Brookes, the gallant appeal of Wilding, the steadiness of William Larned, the flashing serve of Maurice McLoughlin, the fighting determination of Little Bill Johnston, the all-around genius of Tilden, the daring of cat-like Cochet, the deft volley of Richards, the machine-like precision of Rene Lacoste, the brilliant dash of Jean Borotra, the rocketing drives of Ellsworth Vines, the awe-inspiring backhand of Budge, the unbelievable scrambling and retrieving ability of Bitsy Grant, the devastating "big game" of Jack Kramer, and the stupendous, overpowering blasts of Pancho Gonzales. Yes, this breath-taking picture of variety is bound to force you into an incredulous smile. Now top off your visions by adding as a background the shimmering tenseness and butterflies-in-the-stomach feeling associated with any final match, all the way from the local tennis club to the center court at Wimbledon. Thus inspired, you cannot help but resolve to work on, think about and improve every aspect of your style in this wonderful game.

And, finally, you enterprising players should remember, the perfect singles player has not yet walked out on any tennis court!

chapter 2

History —the Great Players

Devotees of lawn tennis can thank a major in the British Army for making the game into a world-wide sport. Tennis is traceable in one form or another all the way back to the ancient Greeks. The Romans played a form of it under the name of "Pila". And the nobles of France developed their own complex version which is now known as court tennis. But the expense of the court for this game made it available to only a limited few. Thus, tennis all but died out in the nineteenth century.

Then along came Major Walton Clopton Wingfield with an idea for a game which he first described to some of his friends in a booklet, "The Major's Game of Lawn Tennis"—dedicated to the party assembled at Nantclwyd in December 1873. The basic inventive thought was to provide a simple, inexpensive court which would make the game available to the public. Major Wingfield applied for a patent on a portable court for playing tennis February 23, 1874. He was awarded Letters Patent No. 685 on July 24, 1874.

The game spread with astounding speed around the world, largely because the British Army adopted it enthusiastically as a barracks exercise. Thus, it appeared in the United States in 1874, India in 1875, Germany in 1876, France in 1877 and Australia in 1878. There have been remarkably few rule changes since these early days; a testimony to the soundness of the game.

The first great singles tournament was organized at Wimbledon in England in 1877. The first champion was Spencer W. Gore. Except for interruptions attributable to war, Wimbledon has been held ever since. This tradition is such a drawing card for players the world over that the tournament is usually considered the world's greatest.

The second most important singles tournament was inaugurated in the United States in 1881. That was the first year the United States National Championship was held by the United States Lawn Tennis Association. The first tournament was held in Newport, Rhode Island, and was won by Richard D. Sears. This great tournament has been staged every year since (except 1917) at various locations such as Newport, Philadelphia and the West Side Tennis Club at Forest Hills, Long Island.

The world's third most famous singles encounter is the outgrowth of an inspired thought by one of the early tennis greats of the United States, Dwight F. Davis. While still a student at Harvard, Davis decided to present a trophy for a series of international team matches between the United States and the British Isles. He selected for his trophy of good will a large and beautiful silver bowl, which promptly became known as the Davis Cup. The importance of the concept was almost immediately expanded beyond the fondest dreams of the youthful Davis. The Davis Cup became a symbol not just of United States vs. Britain, but of international team supremacy as the tennis associations of the world readily adopted the idea. In addition, it became a shining symbol of sportsmanship and of love of the game of tennis. No sports event in history has had such a favorable effect in fostering international good will and understanding as the Davis Cup. Play for the cup consists of a series of elimination rounds involving four singles and one doubles match in each round, with the winner requiring victories in three of the five matches. The nation winning the elimination series then plays the previous year's winner in the Challenge Round for the Davis Cup. Because this great series of matches has brought about competition between the world's best players throughout the years since the initial presentation in 1900, it has played a vital role in the development of the game by singles. By a bit of richly-deserved justice, Davis was himself a member of the first winning team, contributing vital victories for the United States in both singles and doubles! In later life Davis also gained fame as a member of the Cabinet of President Calvin Coolidge.

The records of the nations over the years in Davis Cup Challenge Round competition are shown in Table I. The outstanding singles play of the United States is clearly evident. However, the vital and illuminating fact to note at this moment is that over the past fifteen years Australia has won twelve Challenge Rounds. During this period the fighting Aussies have won forty-three out of sixty singles matches! There is no doubt about it, our youngsters have some real work ahead if they are to regain world tennis supremacy for the United States.

In order to select the top singles players of history, it is necessary to study their records with particular emphasis on the basis of their performances in the three aforementioned events, the Wimbledon, United States and Davis Cup Challenge Round contests. When this is done, it becomes obvious that it is possible to omit from the list certain of the more recent greats because they turned professional after comparatively few key victories. Therefore, it was decided out of fairness, as well as for accuracy, that a fourth criterion for judgment be added. The best measure obtainable for performance by the professionals was that of top annual ranking, as no one or two tournaments appeared to be accepted as representing the championship. With this added factor, a listing of the best singles players of all times has been made, as shown in Table II on the following page.

TABLE I

DAVIS CUP CHALLENGE ROUNDS

Nation	No. of Challenge Rounds	No. of Challenge Rounds Won	No. of Singles Matches Won	Percentage of Singles Matches Won
United States	42	19	81	48
Australia	32	18	65	51
Great Britain	16	9	40	63
France	9	6	19	53
Italy	2	0	1	13
Japan	1	0	0	0
Belgium	1	0	0	0
Mexico	1	0	0	0

From 1877 to date the game of singles has gone through continued development and improvement at the hands of these great players. Valuable assistance has, of course, been rendered by numerous coaches, students of of the game and writers. Deserving of special mention in this category are such people as: Mercer Beasely, Wilfred Baddeley, Teach Tennant, J. Parmly Paret, Harry Hopman, Tom Stow, Dick Skeen, Allison Danzig, Fred Hawthorne and others.

TABLE II

Name and Nationality	Wimbledon	United States	Davis Cup	Ranking Professional
W. Renshaw (G.B.)	81, 82, 83, 84, 85, 86, 89			
R. D. Sears (U.S.)		81, 82, 83, 84, 85, 86, 87		
R. F. Doherty (G.B.)	98, 99, 00		02, 03	
H. L. Doherty (G.B.)	02, 03, 04, 05, 06	03	03(2), 04(2), 05(2), 06(2)	
R. D. Wrenn (U.S.)		93, 94, 96, 97		
M. Whitman (U.S.)		98, 99, 00	00(2), 02(2)	
W. A. Larned (U.S.)		01, 02, 07, 08, 09, 10, 11	02, 03	
N. E. Brookes (A.)	07, 14		07(2), 08, 09(2), 11(2), 12, 14	
A. F. Wilding (A.)	10, 11, 12, 13		07, 08, 09(2)	
W. M. Johnston (U.S.)	23	15, 19	20(2), 21(2), 22(2), 23, 25(2), 26(2)	
M. E. McLoughlin (U.S.)		12, 13	13, 14(2)	
W. T. Tilden (U.S.)	20, 21, 30	20, 21, 22, 23, 24, 25, 29	20(2), 21(2), 22(2), 23(2), 24(2), 25(2), 26, 27, 28, 29, 30	31, 32, 33
J. Borotra (F.)	24, 26		29, 30, 32(2)	
J. R. Lacoste (F.)	25, 28	26, 27	26, 27(2), 28	
H. Cochet (F.)	27, 29	28	27, 28(2), 29(2), 30(2), 31,(2), 32, 33	
H. E. Vines, Jr. (U.S.)	32	31, 32	32	34, 35, 36, 37, 38
F. J. Perry (G.B.)	34, 35, 36	33, 34, 36	33(2), 34(2), 35(2), 36(2)	
J. D. Budge (U.S.)	37, 38	37, 38	37(2), 38(2)	39, 40, 41, 42, 43, 44, 45
R. L. Riggs (U.S.)	39	39, 41	38, 39	46, 47
J. A. Kramer (U.S.)	47	46, 47	46(2), 47(2)	48, 49, 50, 51, 52
F. R. Schroeder, Jr. (U.S.)	49	42	46, 47(2), 48(2), 49(2), 51	
R. A. Gonzales (U.S.)		48, 49	49(2)	53, 54, 55, 56, 57, 58, 59, 60, 61
F. Sedgman (A.)	52	51, 52	50(2), 51(2), 52(2)	
R. G. Laver (A.)	61, 62	62	60(2), 61(2), 62(2)	
R. Emerson (A.)	64	61, 64	61(2), 63(2), 64(2)	

Let us trace the development of the game of singles by running through some of the interesting aspects of history. In this way a clear picture can be gained of the effect of each newly formulated attack and defense on the evolution of singles. While you will find that the game has gone through several phases, there is one solid foundation on which each new forward development is based. That foundation is speed, more and more speed—hitting the ball harder and sooner in order to make the attack more potent and the defense more difficult.

By the time the first Wimbledon tournament began in 1877, the original Marylebone Cricket Club tennis rules formulated in 1875 had been altered. While these changes made the size and shape of the court and the location of service line as we know them today, they left the net high. It was only lowered from the original 4 feet at the center and 5 feet at the sides, to 3 feet 3 inches at the center. The astute Mr. Gore, first Wimbledon champion, used this to advantage by camping at the center of the net and volleying his way to the title. It turned out to be absurdly easy—you see the lob had not yet been invented! But the smarter members of the opposition did just that within the year, and Gore was quickly mastered in what was to prove the first of a long series of see-saw battles between net play and base line play. With the high net, the net player just could not get close enough to the net to volley down effectively without overexposing himself to an easy lob. The most interesting point for the aspiring singles player to note about all of this is that even the very first tennis tournaments were won by the players who used their heads.

The next three years represented the pat ball era supreme. The difficulty of volleying in the face of the high net led to opponents' remaining on the base line. From this position they traded soft, graceful, unhurried shots. Proper manners and dress were the rule of the day.

Then came drama. The Renshaw brothers, William and Ernest, brought volleying back into the picture with a vengeance. To counteract the high net they volleyed from the service line, and to overcome the lob they developed the overhead smash. Against the leisurely base line play of the day this style was murderous. However, at about this moment there arrived on the scene H. F. Lawford, who developed a blistering, topspin drive from the base line. The two styles, volley and overhead vs. improved passing shots, in the persons of W. Renshaw vs. Lawford, fought it out for numerous titles over a period of some eight years. The attributes of their games were debated at length in the press and throughout tennis circles. In 1883, about the middle of the rivalry, the net was officially lowered to its present level of 3 feet in the center and 3 feet 6 inches at the sides. This served to intensify the debate as it seemed bound to affect the outcome of the rivalry. While W. Renshaw had won and continued to win most of the encounters, this did not convince everyone that the net was the place to play. In fact, over the next few years brother E. Renshaw and W. Baddeley vied for the title from the base line, utilizing steady ground strokes.

This sort of tennis threw the game into a brief period of depression as far as spectator appeal was concerned. However, a new fresh wind of gale force was gathering on the horizon in the form of the greatest brother act in tennis history—R. F. and H. L. Doherty. For a decade their outstanding British and Davis Cup play so popularized the game as to assure tennis a role as a leading world sport for many years to come. Reggie (Big Do), two years the senior, and Laurie (Little Do) both went to Cambridge where they were tennis heroes. One year after graduation Reggie won his first Wimbledon title, and the Doherty reign was on. Over the next several years the Dohertys between them won eight Wimbledon singles titles, and Laurie became the first foreigner ever to win the United States championship when he did so in 1903.

What did these brothers possess which permitted them to so dominate play? While they invented little in the way of stroke production, what they did do was to combine abilities in all strokes to a finished perfection which has probably been surpassed to date only by Tilden. Reggie had a flawless, smooth, seemingly effortless stroke and a marvelous sense of anticipation. He could always beat Laurie if he could pick his day, as his one weakness was a physical one brought on by chronic indigestion, making him slow of foot. Reggie, the shorter of the two, had sound strokes of a more severe nature, and covered the court to perfection. They were equally at home in the back court and at net, and were capable of adjusting their games to match any attack or defense they met. They were tacticians by instinct. In short, they brought the first all-court game to tennis. This overwhelming style was to be the model of many greats for years to come. To this they added the court appeal of attractive personalities combined with perfect manners and gallant sportsmanship. This made them the favorites of the large galleries which they attracted wherever they played. Thus did these remarkable brothers contribute immeasurably to the increase in popularity and technical skill of tennis.

Despite the seeming invincibility of the Dohertys, tennis marched onward at the very moment they retired. A new star arose in the person of a great natural athlete from far-off Australia named Norman E. Brookes. A self-taught, heady player, he went all the way to the Wimbledon finals on his first visit to England in 1905 before being beaten by Laurie Doherty.

He never had an opportunity to avenge this defeat. However, it is interesting to note that his famous compatriot, Tony Wilding, while picking H. L. Doherty as the "most graceful and finished player who ever lived", went on to say, "Brookes could beat him at his best." A leftie who relied on accurately placed shots hit with a loosely strung racket; four types of serves, each hit with the same motion; a marvelous volleying touch; classical footwork and daring shots; Brookes was truly described as a tennis wizard. He played top-flight tennis over a seventeen-year span. During this time he acquired such knowledge of the tactics and strokes of the game that the great Tilden was uneasy playing against him, even though their famous meeting was in the twilight of Brookes' career in 1920. As Tilden put it, he felt his game and brain were being picked apart by a calculating genius who eyed every move he made, and then proceeded to produce an answer to each maneuver from his deep store of shots and knowledge. Brookes was a distinguished member of the all-court game school.

The reader has probably noticed that up to this point none of the tennis greats described emanated from the United States. We had developed a number of fine players such as R. D. Sears, Malcolm Whitman and William Larned, but none had quite reached the stature of the Dohertys or Brookes. However, several American players such as O. S. Campbell, Holcombe Ward and B. C. Wright had been experimenting with the serve and volley type of game. While it did not pay off immediately against the all-court game of the previously mentioned greats, it did contribute ultimately to the development of the game of singles. In fact, the next great champion, as if to prove the infinite variety of tennis, was an outright gambler from the wild west who knew only one game serve and volley.

Out of California there roared a grinning, freckle-faced, redheaded kid named Maurice E. McLoughlin. He was destined to become the first tennis hero of the man in the street. It was not just that McLoughlin was the first product of humble surroundings and public park tennis courts to become champion that appealed to the public. It was also the manner in which he achieved his victories. Whatever lingering belief still existed in the minds of the public that tennis was a pantywaist sport was swept away by the blasting racket of the California Comet. Brought up on the fast cement courts of the West, McLoughlin developed a style of brawn and speed aimed at never giving the opponent time to think. He had a lightning serve (figure 2) the likes of which had never been seen before, and he followed almost every one in to the net in order to volley the return. Equipped with only these weapons plus a dogged determination, the popular McLoughlin became the world champion in the 1912-1914 period, beating both

figure 2

Maurice E. McLoughlin

*One of the key inventors in the evolution
of today's brand of attacking tennis is
shown here employing his devastating
serve. Note the all-out effort as he strokes
the ball with every ounce of weight behind
it and, simultaneously, brings his right foot
over the line to begin his sprint toward the
net to reach the volleying position.*

Brookes and Wilding in the Davis Cup. When at the top, the Comet won because his serve could not be broken. He seemed able to pull aces out of the hat when he needed them most. Once when down 10-11, 0-40 to Brookes in a critical Davis Cup match, he served three aces in a row and went on to win the set and match.

This serve and volley game of McLoughlin must be credited as the pioneer version of the so-called big game of today. McLoughlin was not as strong off the ground as many who followed him, so that as soon as opponents learned how to handle his serve, he was quickly dethroned. It is interesting to note that when people like Wilding and R. Norris Williams did beat McLoughlin, they managed to do so by standing in on his serve, taking it on the rise and passing him as he came in to net. This too was the forerunner of a new style that was to lay the foundation for many memorable matches between the top servers and the ground stroke artists.

The tennis era which followed McLoughlin was one that is often termed the golden era of tennis. It was dominated by the development of the all-court game to its ultimate by William T. Tilden and William M. Johnston. For a period stretching over the years from 1915 to 1930 this remarkable pair of tennis players won between them nine U. S. singles titles, four Wimbledon championships, and twenty-nine Davis Cup Challenge Round singles matches! Never before or since has one pair so firmly, artistically, completely, and yet popularly, ruled the tennis world. Johnston, a short, frail man, won the hearts of all who watched him because he possessed the fighting determination and the blasting forehand of a giant. But, despite his marvelous game, Little Bill Johnston could never quite match Big Bill Tilden. They met for the U. S. title six times with Tilden winning five of the celebrated encounters.

In the minds of many students of the game, Tilden was the greatest tennis player who ever walked on a court. It is almost impossible to find a flaw in his game. He had a delivery so fast it became known as the cannonball serve. With it he whipped across aces seemingly at will at crucial points in a match. With his forehand (figure 3) and backhand he could play every type of spin or flat shot, using every change of angle, depth and pace in the books to compel any opponent to play the type of game Tilden had chosen. His lob, especially his overspin variety, was deadly. He would volley with the best. He lived and breathed tennis so that whenever a weakness showed up in his game he would practice untold hours until he conquered it completely. And he had the courage, stamina and amazing longevity of reign of the true champion. The longevity was all the more

figure 3

William T. (Big Bill) Tilden

The great master is shown here—at the peak of his career—as he moves flawlessly into position for a forehand drive. Note in particular his attention on the ball, fluidity of motion and perfect balance as he sprints toward the point of impact. The racket is starting back high in the manner of many great forehands.

remarkable because he was twenty-seven before winning his first U. S. title—an age when most singles players are past their peak. Finally, Tilden had that indescribable bearing of a tennis great which tends to make an opponent feel as though he does not even belong on the same court. Merely his decision to enter or not to enter a tournament created international incidents requiring the attention of kings and presidents. Truly he deserves the rating of a tennis genius, and the accolade for having contributed most to the development of tennis since the introduction of the game.

Many times Tilden delighted in playing against the strong points of an opponent just to prove he could beat him at his own game. With his amazing versatility he could outdrive a William Johnston, outchop a Wallace Johnson and even outsteady a Bitsy Grant from the base line on a clay court! At times he had streaks of tennis so devastating that those who watched still remember as if it were yesterday. Perhaps the two most celebrated such streaks were when he beat Wallace Johnson in the 1921 finals of the U. S. Nationals 6-1, 6-3, 6-1 in 45 minutes, and when he flawlessly mastered the great Manuel Alonso 6-0, 6-0, 6-2 at Forest Hills in 1923.

Defeat, the ultimate fate of all champions, finally came to Tilden through the efforts of two French masters, Rene Lacoste and Henri Cochet. The interesting point is that they posssessed widely differing games, and used quite different tactics to beat Tilden. Lacoste was a tennis machine of tremendous precision who got everything back with enough pace on the ball to keep the pressure on his opponent. Mixed in were short shots which forced Tilden to run in to net against his will. In this way he tired the aging Tilden as he waited for his opportunity to take advantage of an opening. Cochet, on the other hand, played a new dashing-and-daring type of game reminiscent of R. Norris Williams. He decided that the evolution of tennis lay in the direction of greater speed in the rallies. Thus, he took every ball on the rise or volleyed it in order to hurry Tilden on every shot and prevent him from getting set to make the type of return he wished. A favorite Cochet maneuver was to draw Tilden out of position by hitting a short, sharply-angled shot, play the return for the opening created and then take the net to volley the next one for the point. Cochet was short, graceful and speedy. He possessed fine ground strokes hit with a short, flat swing which disguised direction up to the moment of impact. But it was his volley and half volley for which he was so well known and which, like Vincent Richards, he often hit from the middle of the court. While he was criticized for this particular tactic, it is interesting to note that his principle of playing the ball as early as possible in order to keep the opponent off balance has since been universally adopted. As earlier predicted by McLoughlin, Brookes and Tilden, not one great champion since Cochet has played anything but the faster game with emphasis on the forecourt attack.

As we shall see, the move toward the present ultimate forecourt attack, the big game, took about twenty years. Of the celebrated Four Musketeers, Lacoste, Cochet, Borotra and Jacques Brugnon, only Borotra utilized the serve and volley game. However, the development of this attack had not quite reached the point where Borotra, with his unorthodox strokes, could conquer the all-court games of Tilden, Cochet and Lacoste. This great French Dynasty held sway over the tennis world about seven years. It was finally broken by a lanky kid named H. Ellsworth Vines.

Vines had only a brief, meteoric career as an amateur, but then went on to dominate the pro ranks for five years. His game was the all-court variety built around an absolutely devastating serve hit with picturesque coordination, coupled with perhaps the most severe forehand in the history of the game. Cochet, whom Vines finally blasted right off the top of the international scene, once recorded an eloquent description of Vines' serve as follows: "No serve had the coordination of movement, vigor and suppleness of Vines." In serving a match point at Wimbledon against Cochet, legend has it that Vines hit his flat delivery ace so hard that Cochet never saw the ball and had to await the umpire's announcement of the score to learn he had lost the match. The flat, blistering forehands of Vines were hit with the same small margin of error as his serves. Depending on his touch, and the condition of his unfortunately sensitive stomach, Vines could be merely good or just about unbeatable in his day. Certainly his fast, uncompromising game drew the admiration of the galleries and inspired many younger players.

The next dominant figure in singles was a natural, marvelously coordinated athlete—an Englishman named Fred Perry, who was also tops as a ping-pong player. He was noted for his running forehand which he followed in to net to take the attacking position. Although he may not have realized it at the time, this maneuver had quite an influence on the subsequent development of the blossoming big game of the Americans. In studying Perry, they decided the only way to beat him was to take the net at every opportunity

The player who did so was a gangling, unassuming, extremely popular, reddish-haired youngster from California named J. Donald Budge. The possessor of a powerful, all-court game, Budge was noted primarily for his backhand. This shot, normally the weakest part of any tennis player's game, was a vision of smooth, overwhelming power when stroked by

Budge. He made it into an attacking weapon which he utilized to become in 1938 the first—and, to date, the only—player to win the singles championship of England, France, the United States and Australia in the same year. Following this he went on to rule the professional ranks for seven years. Recognized by many as second only to Tilden among U. S. tennis greats, it may well be that history will credit him more in the future as having been the instigator of the transition from the all-court game to the so-called big game of today.

Against the usual opponent Budge—like his idol, Vines—just hit harder and deeper, took the net only as needed and literally blew the victim off the court. There was no subtlety, no planning, no smart strategy—just overwhelming power. But there were times against Perry and Von Cramm when Budge had to resort to other tactics. A typical example occurred in the previously mentioned Davis Cup victory over Von Cramm. After being down 1-4 in the fifth set, Budge, with his back to the wall, changed his game and took the net at every opportunity, both on serve and return of service. His backhand return of service, which he hit on the rise as he came in, was one of the truly picture-book shots of all times. This type of power-laden net attack (see figure 4) was the only way you could beat an inspired all-court player like Perry or Von Cramm.

Now this, as is the case with most things in tennis, was not a brand new thought. As early as 1893, James Dwight was pointing out the value of the attack when he wrote: "There is a great moral effect in being always on the offensive. If you stay back your opponent can place his stroke where he pleases, but if you go forward he has got to avoid you, and may very easily lose the stroke in trying to do so." Examples of attacking types of games have been fairly numerous from the outset. Gore, the first champion, was an attack-minded volleyer, and so were such greats as W. Renshaw, O. S. Campbell, Maurice McLoughlin, and Jean Borotra. But none could match the power and perfection of the modern big game as developed through extension of Budge's game by Kramer and Gonzales.

John A. Kramer, another Californian, followed Budge as the dominant figure in tennis. At first he utilized a marvelously graceful, flawless and powerful all-court game to sweep all before him in the amateur ranks in 1946 and 1947. He then turned professional and ruled this game another five years. It was during this time that he developed the modern game of singles, known as the big game. On a fast court it is so overwhelming that all great modern players have been forced to adopt it as a model. Benefiting from the aforementioned development of the pressing attack as contributed by Budge, Kramer went a step beyond and attacked every second.

figure 4

J. Donald Budge

Shown here—at the peak of his career—blasting an overhead in characteristic form is the great Don Budge. Note the familiar scissor kick off the right foot which permits him to go high in the air. The racket is almost flat, as it is caught just as the follow-through starts. Body position and balance are perfect.

There was absolutely no compromise. Both first and second serves were followed in to the net. The power he generated, coupled with the speed, agility, reach, volley and overhead capabilities he developed, made it practically impossible to break his service. In fact it was seldom that an opponent could win more than one point a game against his serve as placements streamed off his racket. His receiving tactics were just as unmerciful. He stood in close, took the ball on the rise and went to the net whenever possible in order to engineer a break. All of the previous ideas of uncompromising speed were brought to a peak in his style of play to the extent that Kramer's placements often outnumbered the sum of his nets and outs! Even the oldest of tennis critics were forced to admit that this style of play was the most devastating ever witnessed. Every ball he hit felt like a hunk of lead as it came off the ground. Without doubt, Big Jake made a lasting contribution to the development of tennis.

It seems as though it takes a Californian to beat a Californian, and the most recent great champion is no exception. Out of nowhere in 1948 an unranked kid named Richard A. Gonzales rocketed to the championship of the United States. After a brief, two-year career at the top of the amateur ranks, he turned professional. Under the expert tutelage of Kramer, his rather spotty big game turned into a vision of annihilation even for an atomic age. Once Pancho Gonzales learned to take full advantage of his marvelous physique and natural abilities, he became unconquerable. Endowed with cat-like speed, with which to maneuver his athletic seventy-four-inch frame, and a real killer instinct, he was an apt pupil. By 1953 he unseated Kramer to become the top professional and he has remained on the throne for nine consecutive years. To accomplish this domination he utilizes exclusively the big game of the Kramer school. His serve is even more powerful than Kramer's and the balance of his game almost as well-rounded, in that he can also make every shot in the books. To break his serve on a fast court is close to impossible. His speed and reflexes are so fast that he literally blankets the net as he follows in behind every serve to volley away any returns for amazingly routine placements. Whereas many of the former champions rested in certain games and were even content to throw sets, the physical conditioning of the Kramer-Gonzales school is such that they go all out for every point without letup. This results in terrific pressure applied without quarter, which serves to further emphasize the true quality of the big game.

That brings us up to date and thus completes the story of the outstanding male tennis players. Before an analysis is made in an attempt to compare various players, it is only proper to have a look at the fairer sex. After all,

TABLE III

Outstanding Women Singles Players

Name and Nationality	Tournament and Year of Victory	
	Wimbledon	United States
Mrs. Blanche Bingley Hillyard (G.B.)	1886, 89, 94, 97, 99, 1900	
Lottie Dod (G.B.)....................................	1887, 88, 91, 92, 93	
Mrs. Charlotte Cooper Sterry (G.B.)	1895, 96, 98, 1901, 08	
Mrs. Dorothy Douglass Chambers (G.B.)	1903, 04, 06, 10, 11, 13, 14	
May G. Sutton (U.S.).............................	1905, 07	1904
Mrs. Hazel H. Wightman (U.S.)..............		1909, 10, 11, 19
Mrs. Molla B. Mallory (U.S.)..................		1915, 16, 17, 18, 20, 21, 22, 26
Suzanne Lenglen (F.)	1919, 20, 21, 22, 23, 25	
Mrs. Helen Wills Moody (U.S.).............	1927, 28, 29, 30, 32, 33, 35, 38	1923, 24, 25, 27, 28, 29, 31
Helen Jacobs (U.S.)................................	1936	1932, 33, 34, 35
Alice Marble (U.S.)................................	1939	1936, 38, 39, 40
Pauline Betz (U.S.)..................................	1946	1942, 43, 44, 46
Mrs. Margaret Osborne duPont (U.S.)....	1947	1948, 49, 50
A. Louise Brough (U.S.).........................	1948, 49, 50	1947, 52, 53
Maureen Connolly (U.S.)........................	1952, 53	1951, 52, 53
Maria E. Bueno (Brazil)	1959, 60, 64	1959, 63, 64

we must never forget that it was an enterprising girl named Mary Outerbridge who first brought tennis to the United States in 1874. Of interest is that the source of the tennis equipment she obtained was a friend in the British Army stationed in Bermuda.

The records of the outstanding women singles players are presented in Table III. The first women's singles championship was held at Wimbledon in 1884, seven years after the inauguration of the men's tournament. The first winner was Miss Maud Watson. Through the years this tournament has been considered the top event for the ladies. The only other which ranks close to this one in importance is the United States championship. This tournament was begun in 1887 and was first won by Ellen F. Hansell. The play of the pioneers in the game was distinctly handicapped by an overwhelming modesty which required playing in hat, dress, petticoats and the works. As the girls became more willing to expose their knees in public, the pace of their tennis increased markedly. So, incidentally, did the interest of the galleries.

The most famous of the women players around the turn of the century were May Sutton and Hazel H. Wightman, who did much to train youngsters and popularize the game. Mrs. Wightman also stimulated international competition by presenting in 1923 the famed Wightman Cup, for which the ladies of England and the United States compete each year. To celebrate the first competition, Mrs. Wightman earned a point for the United States by winning her doubles match.

The next era was a golden one for women's tennis. A bombshell burst on the scene in the person of a vivacious, young French girl named Suzanne Lenglen. Trained since early childhood and speedy afoot, Lenglen swept the tennis world before her with her accurately hit shots. Legend has it that she could place any of her deep or favorite soft, widely-angled shots on a handkerchief. Her lively temperament was akin to that of an opera star, and wherever she played she not only attracted the galleries but also stole the headlines. Thus, she contributed mightily to bringing the women's game to the attention of the public. Many of those who followed her career thought she was the greatest of all the women players. Unfortunately she was never seen at her best by her fans in the United States, losing to Molla B. Mallory, the perennial U.S. champion, at Forest Hills in 1921.

The next great champion in this era was the complete opposite of Mlle. Lenglen. Helen Wills Moody was a serious, mechanical player who showed so little emotion that she was immediately named "Little Miss Poker Face" by the press. Behind that unruffled expression was a concentration and determination seldom seen in any tennis player. This, coupled with a depth and pace in her ground game as yet unmatched in women's tennis, carried her to the most remarkable string of victories ever won by a tennis player. From the start to finish of a match she kept such a tactically well planned and relentless pressure on her opponent that she won eight Wimbledon and seven United States championships over a fifteen year span! Despite the fact that the men rightly tend to look down upon the game of the weaker sex, any male player the world over is willing to tip his hat to this amazing record.

Following Queen Suzanne and Queen Helen, the great ladies have adopted the teachings of the men and tend more and more to take the net and volley for the kill. Examples of this advanced technique include first of all Alice Marble. The possessor of a fine athletic build and natural ability, Marble was able to play the male style of forcing game as well as any girl before or since. She served and volleyed with real power, and covered the court well. Her contemporaries ranked her as the best ever among the women. The two most noteworthy singles players since Marble are Pauline Betz and Maureen Connolly. Betz was known largely for her fine backhand and her fighting qualities. And Connolly, better known as "Little Mo", after the battleship U. S. S. Missouri, was renowned for her solid, bombarding type of base line, driving game. Her short stature prevented her from developing a serving, net-rushing game. The latest addition to the greats is Maria Bueno, the graceful Brazilian with a classic all-court game and breathtaking touch.

In general, the ladies play a type of singles which is a notch well below that of the men, as they cannot hit as severely or cover the court as well. Thus, they have not contributed greatly to the development of the game from a technical standpoint. Instead, they tend to follow the lead of the males.

Let us now return to the most controversial portion of any tennis history —that of comparing the old timers with the modern players. Most writers accept the better part of valor and claim that it is impossible to compare a Doherty, Whitman, Brookes, McLoughlin, Larned, Tilden, Johnston, Lacoste, Cochet, Vines, Perry, Budge or Kramer with a Gonzales. We would like to deviate from this practice of the past fifty years.

There is no doubt that the game of tennis, like all sports, has improved with time. The modern game, just as predicted by many former greats, is a game in which speed is king. The player must plan further ahead, think quicker, hit sooner and move faster under greater pressure than ever before. In addition, the improved tennis racket, balls and clothes add to the speed of the game.

Beyond any question, the big game as played today far outstrips any all-court game of the past. Does this mean that the more modern players, Kramer and Gonzales, are head-and-shoulders above Tilden as tennis players? We would like to answer this question in two ways. First, we believe that a Kramer or Gonzales employing the big game of today would consistently beat a Tilden on grass playing his all-court game of 1920-1925. Second, we are convinced that had Tilden lived in the 1960 era, he likewise would have adopted and mastered the big game style. So equipped, the Tilden of 1960 could have murdered the Tilden of 1920-1925. There is no denying the remarkable skills of the greats of the past, but a Doherty of 1900 could provide little competition for a Doherty of 1960. We agree, however, that it is impossible to compare accurately a Tilden, Budge or Kramer employing the 1960 style of tennis with a Gonzales of 1960.

Yes, tennis has made great forward strides since 1874. The development of the game has been entirely logical and consistent. And the best is yet to come.

the
Game

In the first and second chapters it has been stated in various ways that tennis is an intellectual game of high order. And yet some of the top players have not been noted for their strategic powers—indeed some have even written that they never think on the court. What is the explanation?

We have not wished or intended to frighten the beginner, club player or even the seasoned tournament circuit player by overemphasizing the complexities of tennis. While the game *is* truly complex, it is at the same time possible to simplify your play by developing at the outset a sound knowledge and understanding of the fundamentals. Such comprehension permits you to play the proper shot, in the most effective manner, at the right moment, almost automatically or intuitively. This is certainly what the champions do, and it explains why some evidently do not realize they are thinking while on the court. They exhibit an uncanny instinct to make the correct shot—but do not overlook the fact that this ability was developed through many hours of practice, coaching, study and tournament experience.

There is another important part to the explanation of the seeming lack of strategic powers of some of the tennis greats. From time to time there appears on the scene a champion so outstanding that he just overpowers all the opposition. This was certainly the case for Helen Wills Moody and Don Budge when they were at the top of their careers—they took control of every match by just hitting so hard and so deep that they did not have to resort to brilliant tactical variations. In others words, superior stroke production minimizes the necessity for imaginative strategy. However, even in the case of a Moody or a Budge, age finally begins to show its effect on pace and at this point you will find that these fine players depended on more study and on-court thinking to maintain their superiority.

Now the major purpose of this book is to provide an exposition of the fundamentals of tennis from the standpoint of both tactics and stroke production so that the reader can learn to do the right thing at the right time. As this skill is developed, you can learn to do certain basic things essentially automatically in order to be able to concentrate your thinking on the more subtle factors. You will discover that this will have a tremendous effect on your ability to overcome your own weaknesses and to exploit those of your opponent.

In this chapter we will attempt to present an over-all picture of the game of singles as obtained through extensive study of actual matches, and to introduce the basic aspects of stroke production.

Before launching into details, something must be said about types of tennis courts, since this is an important consideration in determining the style of play. It may seem unbelievable, but a change in speed of bounce of a fraction of a second can and does make a big difference in the type of tennis game which should be played. Tennis courts can be ranked in terms of speed as follows: board, hard court such as cement or asphalt, grass, composition and, finally, clay as the slowest of all. For practical purposes, a division can be made at the point of grass, so that all matches played on grass or above can be called fast courts. Since most important tournaments are played on fast courts, the emphasis in the development of tennis has, as already shown in chapter 2, been in the direction of more and more speed. This explains to a large degree the birth of the big game. Therefore, this chapter will be devoted largely to tactics of the fast court game, and will then deal more briefly with the slower, clay court game.

An over-all examination of the game of singles indicates that the four major factors in building a sound game are:

Offense

Modern singles is definitely a game of offensive play. The offense is composed of serve and net play, and between them, these two factors account for two thirds of all the winning shots in singles. The big serve, the hard-punched volley and the solid overhead are the hallmarks of today's best players. This emphasis on attack is not to belittle the requirement for sound ground strokes—one must also possess these in order to be truly great.

Anticipation

Once the serve has been hit and the server follows it in to net, the struggle for the point revolves around the effectiveness of the volleys of the server and the passing shots of the receiver. Anyone who has tried to cover a 27-foot-wide tennis net against first-rate passing shots realizes the amazing speed and agility which must be developed by the net players. In order to volley offensively it is absolutely essential that the net player develop his anticipatory powers to a superb degree. You have to be moving in the right direction at the proper split second, or you are a goner. This means you have to know where each return is going by studying the position of the ball with respect to the player, position of the player's feet, racket and wrist for various shots, and his habits under various tactical situations.

By the same token, the receiver, in order to have a chance to break service with his passing shots, must be able to anticipate the moves of the net player and the depth and direction of his volleys. In addition, he must be able to hide his intentions to the last moment in order to fool the net player.

Concentration

To maintain the continuous application of power, speed, endurance and tactical generalship required in top-flight singles play necessitates the utmost in concentration. In the game of today there is no place for a let-down in concentration with its consequent release of pressure on the opponent. The pendulum of play can swing rapidly against you. To convince you of the importance of this, here are just a few celebrated examples: Wilding was once down to William Clothier two sets and 2-5, 15-40 in the third set, but gained a respite and won 12-10 in the fifth set. Tilden once lost to Watson Washburn when he got upset over a call while holding a lead of 6-0, 6-1, 4-4 and was about to break Washburn's serve at 30-40. Wallace Johnson was once down 1-5, 15-40 in the deciding set and made a sensational passing shot to save match point while on his knees after slipping down. This broke the concentration of his opponent and Johnson finally won 17-15. In the finals of the 1949 U.S. Championship Ted Schroeder won the first two sets from Gonzales 18-16, 0-2, but let down a bit in the third set. Big Pancho won this at 6-1 and so regained his confidence and touch that he went on to win the championship 6-2, 6-4.

So, it is well to take the advice of the great Tony Wilding who said, "Never relax for a second no matter what the score—the body will usually respond if you have will power, pluck and determination to spur yourself to fresh efforts."

Concentration also demands continued thought aimed at diagnosing weaknesses in the armor of the opponent's game. This entails study while watching him play others as well as during the match. It is priceless information at crucial moments to know the types of shots which are most likely to draw errors from your opponents, and when you are in a hole to know the favorite shots of your opponent so that you can pull off surprising gets. All players have both weaknesses and favorite shots, so that concentration will surely reveal ways and means to pick up vital points.

Determination

Closely linked to concentration as a must in top singles players is the invaluable asset called determination. It is that hard-to-define extra in the makeup of a tennis player which permits him to lift his game at the precise moment of crisis so that he can go on to win. It is an interesting and rare quality that stamps the local as well as the national champion. Just stop and consider how often you have heard people classify players into two groups—those who will not be beaten and those who do not quite have the will to win.

Determination is a lot of things. It is not just trying hard for each point in a match. It also means the willingness to face untold hours of practicing to correct your weaknesses, the courage to come from behind and the control of temperament and wits even under the most adverse conditions. It means developing that proper delicate balance between confidence—which is essential to—and overconfidence—which is poisonous to—top performance.

Tables IV, V and VI present an over-all picture of the numbers of various types of strokes played and their relative importance in producing winners on fast courts. These data were collected from a large number of matches involving top-flight professional and amateur players. The importance of the forcing game, as shown by the frequency and lethality of net play, is worthy of note.

TABLE IV
Fast Courts

Number and Percentile Frequency of Stroke Types During Complete Singles Matches

(Omitting Errors)

	First Service	Second Service	Return of Service	Net Shots				Base Line Shots		
				First Volley	Later Volley	Over-head	Ground Stroke	Passing	Lob	S
No.	583	301	609	423	170	29	13	224	50	2
%	24.5	13	25	18	7	1	0.5	9	2	

30

TABLE V

Number and Percentile Frequency of

Point-Winning Stroke Types

	First Service	Second Service	Return of Service	Net Shots				Base Line Shots		Total Winners
				First Volley	Later Volley	Over-head	Ground Stroke	Passing	Lob	
o.	202	85	180	145	112	27	13	76	23	863
	23	10	21	17	13	3	1	9	3	

TABLE VI

Fast Courts

Relative Probability of Winning a Point with a Given Type of Stroke

Considering the Frequency of the Stroke Utilized

Stroke	Potency Factor	
Overhead	3.9	
Ground stroke at net	2.6	
Later volley	2.4	
Lob	1.9	
Passing shot	1.3	
First service	1.2	
First volley	1.2	
Return of service	1.1	
Second service	1	(basis of comparison)

31

Let us turn our attention to play on the slower tennis courts of the composition or clay variety. Unlike doubles, which is the same game irrespective of surface, singles on a slow court is vastly different from singles on a fast court.

To prove the point, data were taken on matches involving the same players on both grass and composition courts. To nail the differences down beyond question, Gonzales and Lew Hoad were chosen for the comparison since these expert exponents of the big game could play the same devastating game on a slow court if anyone could. However, the data, as recorded in Table VII, show a contrast in tactics which is truly striking.

Referring to Table VII, it is to be expected that the service would be more effective on the faster court, and this is shown to be the case. The really amazing difference, however, is the net play. On grass both players followed 100 per cent of their serves in to the net and achieved 18 per cent of the winners by putting away the first volley. On the slower composition courts they were able to follow in to net only 15 to 20 per cent of their serves and to win only 2 per cent of points of first volleys! The fact that later volleys produced about the same number of winners means that advances to the net were engineered largely by forcing ground strokes on the slower courts rather than via the serve. If one omits serve and return of serve, which must be played from the base line according to the rules, on grass 75 per cent of all points were won at net, while on composition courts only 40 per cent were won at net. Furthermore, while on grass not one single point was won with ground strokes in base line rallies, on composition courts 22 per cent of all points were won in this manner with both players on the base line!

TABLE VII
Percentile Comparison of Winning Points by Gonzales and Hoad on Grass and on Composition Courts

	First Service	Second Service	Return of Service	First Volley	Later Volley	Over-head	At Net	Passing Shot	Base Line Rally	Lob
								Ground Strokes		
Grass Court..	28	8	15	18	12	2	4	10	0	3
Composition Court	18	3	13	2	16	7	3	13	22	3

Percentile Comparison of Winning Points by Modern Players

	First Service	Second Service	Return of Service	First Volley	Later Volley	Over-head	At Net	Passing Shot	Base Line Rally	Lob
Grass Court..	23	10	21	17	13	3	1	9	0	3
Clay Court....	16	8.5	18.5	14	11.5	2	3	16.5	7	3

What all of this means is that with a slower, higher bounce the defender has not only a better opportunity to reach a forcing shot, but also sufficient time to make an effective return. This gain in time of the order of slightly less than a second means from 5 to 10 feet of court coverage depending on whether the defender is standing or running. Such coverage blunts the weapons of the best attackers and makes it possible for a Bitsy Grant to beat them all on clay. The ability to cover court and the possession of sound ground strokes are invaluable assets to the clay court players.

In fact, we would like to contradict certain statements made about the superiority of the big game players at the close of chapter 2. Most of the modern serve and volley greats do not possess the sound, deep ground strokes to permit them to excel on a slow court.

An indication of this is shown in the bottom part of Table VII which compares current grass court and clay court play, data for the latter having been collected at the U. S. National Clay Court Championship in 1958. Note that most of the modern players play the slow court more like the fast court game than do Gonzales and Hoad. Lacking ground strokes, they tend to employ the only attack they know—serve and volley. But justice and sound tactics do finally prevail. The ultimate winner of the 1958 tourney, Bernard Bartzen, was the sole competitor equipped with and utilizing a well-rounded, all-court game.

It is our opinion that many of the greats of the past with their astounding all court prowess, depth, speed, angles, spins, changes of pace, clever tactics and remarkable ability to keep the ball in play, could administer a terrific beating to the current crop of big game boys on clay. Yes, we would have to side with players of the Tilden, Lacoste, Cochet, Grant, Frank Parker and Bobby Riggs type as superior to present-day players on a slow court.

First Fundamentals of Stroke Production

Man has for many centuries used the familiar motions involved in swinging a club and throwing a rock. Swinging a tennis racket is so similar to these natural movements that anyone can play the game.

The basic fundamentals of stroke production are essentially simple motions involving body balance, weight distribution and transfer as the stroke evolves. The payoff on a good tennis stroke, as with a good boxing punch, depends on uncoiling at the correct second just the proper amount of power of the body and throwing it behind the shot. This requires coordination of feet, knees, hips, shoulders and arms. The degree of coordination and split-second timing achieved through long hours of practice by the top players is indeed remarkable. Just as in golf and in baseball, there is in tennis more than one way to hit a ball, but there is also a generally accepted method which most teachers use.

The first thing to consider is how to grip the racket. There are three acceptable means of gripping the racket which are identified as the eastern, western and continental grips.

The safest and most popular grip is the eastern. It is used by most of the hard hitting top players and recent champions such as Vines, Budge, Kramer and Gonzales. The eastern grip actually involves two grips for greater power—one for the forehand and one for the backhand and serve. These grips as used by Budge are illustrated below (figure 5). The only variations in this grip among the top players are in the spread of the fingers caused by individual hand size, racket handle size and comfort. Notice that the face of the racket and the palm of the hand are in the same hitting plane, and there is practically no broken line at the wrist. This grip provides power as the racket, arm and elbow work as one piece—like an iron shaft.

forehand

Shaking hands with the racket is a good way to assume this grip, making sure the handle extends behind the heel of the hand.

backhand

Hand on top of racket with the V between thumb and forefinger pointing to the left shoulder at impact is the proper position for this grip—also used for serve. For ground strokes extend thumb back of handle for support.

figure 5

The continental grip is the same for forehand and backhand. It is taken by grasping the racket as for the eastern forehand and twisting the racket about a quarter turn to the right so that the palm is virtually on top of the racket and the thumb extends across the front of the handle. This was the grip used by the great Fred Perry. It has both advantages and disadvantages. The main advantage is in volleying, since one does not have to change grips, which is most helpful in rapid volley exchanges. It is, therefore, used by many of the top doubles players. It is also effective for chop and slice strokes. However, the experts avoid teaching beginners this grip because on most ground strokes it makes greater demands on controlling the head of the racket with the wrist. This increases the margin for error and demands a strong wrist.

The western grip is taken by placing the racket flat on the ground and picking it up, or by taking the eastern forehand grip and twisting the racket about a quarter turn to the left so that the palm of the hand is behind the racket handle. This grip became popular in California where most of the play is on hard surface courts and the ball takes a high bounce. The master proponent of this grip was Little Bill Johnston, shown in figure 6 walloping his famous forehand. Johnston did not change his grip for his backhand, but stroked the ball on backhand shots with the same face of the racket with which he hit his forehands. This made for a rather awkward looking circular swing in front of the body, but Little Bill worked it with near perfection. While there may be a slight advantage in the western grip in hitting high balls, it represents an exploitable weakness on grass and clay courts where the bounce is lower.

With all these grips the method of hitting a tennis ball can vary. There are those like Bill Johnston and Don McNeil who start with the racket head well below the ball and impart top spin to both forehand and backhand. There are others like Ken Rosewall who start with the racket head fairly high and hit under the ball imparting controlled underspin. Still others such as Vines hit very flat drives.

While the proper grip is important to good tennis, it is not as formalized as correct footwork and body position. Concentrate on learning proper balance while getting your racket back early, face slightly open, and hitting with a natural, relaxed baseball swing with knees bent. Remember each stroke involves four phases—anticipation, preparation, execution and return to position. Always relax the grip between shots to avoid tiring the hand and arm.

The various strokes will be further described in connection with the chapters on serve, return of service, net and base line play.

figure 6

William M. (Little Bill) Johnston

The greatest exponent of the western grip is shown here during the follow-through of his famous forehand drive. Note carefully the physical effort and concentration which allowed the frail Johnston to produce one of the greatest forehands of all time. The hand on top of the racket handle and the angle of the racket face illustrate perfectly the western style.

the

Serve

In this era of offensive tennis the value of the serve can hardly be overemphasized. It is the stroke which permits the striker to gain the all-important advantage of attack at the start of each point. The serve is the most frequently used stroke in championship singles, representing 37.5 per cent of all strokes as shown in Table IV. It also accounts for 33 per cent of all the winning strokes (Table V). These are really impressive numbers! However, the true importance of the serve goes well beyond even these figures. The reason for this is that the serve is also responsible in good measure for many points won later by volleying. This comes about because the serve often draws a weak return, or forces the opponent out of position, thus setting the stage for a winning volley. Therefore, one can say that in championship play on a fast court the serve is directly or indirectly responsible for winning about 40 per cent of all points! No wonder it is usually considered the most important single stroke.

Even on a slow court there is no doubt of the vital role of the serve. While, as would be expected, the effectiveness of the serve is reduced, it still accounts for 21 per cent of winners outright (Table VII). The slower-bounding ball on a composition court also means that the service will lose some of its indirect effect, since the striker cannot often risk following his serve in to net. Now, if we allow some small number to represent indirect benefit, we can use Table VII to get a comparative value of the service on fast and slow courts. When this is done, it shows the big serves of Gonzales and Hoad are about *twice* as effective on grass as on composition! Information of this sort is invaluable when deciding your serving tactics on a given surface. For example, expending energy banging a cannonball serve makes far more sense on grass than on a damp clay court.

Tilden has said the perfect service is 40 per cent placement, 40 per cent speed and 20 per cent spin. But the expert server has to possess brains as well as brawn. Not only must he be able to employ the weapons of spin, speed and placement, but, in addition, he must utilize variety and develop the capability of diagnosing the likes, dislikes and habits of his opponent. Often the server can catch a receiver slightly out of position and slip in a shot which he cannot return effectively, if at all. Other times the server can note on the part of the receiver a weakness against some type of spin, or a tendency under certain circumstances to take unnecessary chances, or to get careless or to let down the slightest bit. To learn and be able to take advantage of such valuable bits of information at crucial points in a match gives the server a most comforting feeling. It builds that all-important ingredient called confidence.

Fast Court Play

The server has three major objectives: (1) He must put the ball into play in a manner aimed at gaining the offense by forcing the receiver into making a weak return or forcing him out of position. (2) He must follow in behind serve to the net position. (3) He must study the receiver during his run to the net position in order to anticipate the type, speed and direction of the return of service.

First let us consider the aim points for first serves as shown in figure 7. The preferred spots are numbered in order of priority from 1 to 3 for both courts. Some 50 per cent of serves to the forehand court are aimed at area 1. The reason for this is to force the receiver out of position and wide of the court, thus opening up almost the whole court for an easy winning volley hit down the other side. (More will be said about the volley in chapter 6—Net Play.) This advantage outweighs the disadvantages of hitting to the receiver's stronger forehand side plus giving him a wider angle for his return of service. About 30 per cent of serves are hit to area 2 because the backhand side is usually the weaker and the receiver will make more errors or poor returns. This is actually the case, as deep serves to area 2 draw about about 40 per cent errors while those to area 1 draw about 30 per cent. The final aim point, area 3, is the target about 7 per cent of the time, with the rest of the court receiving the remaining 13 per cent in random fashion. Area 3 is a favorite aim point when the server possesses a vicious slice delivery. The objective of the server, you will remember, is to grab the offensive. Therefore, the good player keeps moving the ball around to keep the receiver guessing and to throw him off balance. You should watch the opponent carefully to see where he stands and how he moves, in order to take maximum advantage of any openings. For example, if the receiver moves a bit close to the center, a slice serve to aim point 3 is very effective.

Aim Points for First Serves

The preferred aim points for first serves, numbered in order of preference, are shown in the diagram. Serves to the forehand court are made from A_1, and serves to the backhand court from A_2. The favorite aim point, used in at least half the cases, is deep to the outside corner. The reasoning behind this is that it forces the receiver far out of position, opening up the whole court for a winning first volley by the server. The other aim points are used to keep the receiver guessing, to capitalize on a stroke weakness of his or to take advantage of his being out of proper receiving position.

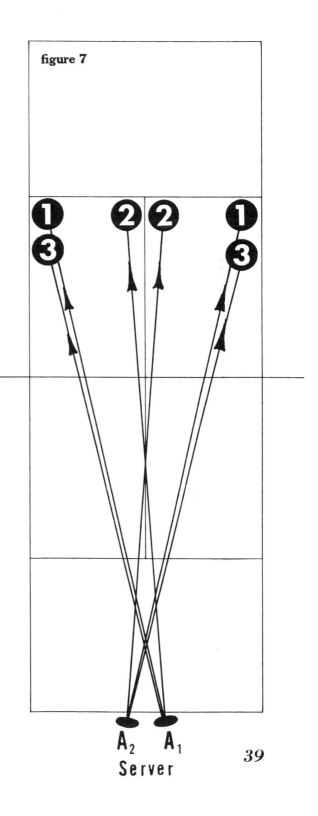

figure 7

A_2 A_1

Server

The favorite first serve to the backhand court is, by the same token, deep at the side line to area 1 in order to move the opponent out of position. Since this also has the added advantage of being hit to the weaker backhand side, it is used as the aim point almost habitually, actually in 56 per cent of the cases. Area 2 deep on the forehand side is the target for about 30 per cent of the serves to keep the receiver honest. Also the forehand is not quite so dangerous on this side since it will be hit from near the middle of the court, where the angle for passing the net-rushing server is a minimum. Some 10 per cent of serves fall in area 3 and the remaining 4 per cent are scattered around. In exceptional cases there are players like Ken Rosewall, whose forehand return of serve is less effective than the backhand. His smarter opponents exploit this fact. For example, in a match which was monitored it was found that Frank Sedgman aimed some 80 per cent of his first serves against Rosewell to area 2. In another era McLoughlin always served to the center against Wilding.

The reason for placing the big serves deep (defined as within 4 feet of the service line) in the corners is readily apparent when one considers the payoff. From one third to one half of such serves are not returned, and the server ultimately wins some 70 to 77 per cent of points which begin in this manner. Clearly, the big first serve is a must for top-flight singles today. The best servers get about 70 per cent of first serves in, of which some 85 per cent are deep. In one match we saw Gonzales get a staggering 86 per cent of all first serves in when serving to the backhand court. This is what makes him so hard to beat.

The aim points for second serves are quite different in order of priority, as shown in figure 8. In the forehand court some 60 per cent of serves are aimed at areas 1 and 2, and about 15 per cent at area 3. In the backhand court about 75 per cent are aimed at areas 1 and 2, and only a sprinkling at area 3 and others. There are sound reasons for this marked preference to serve to the backhand side with the second ball. First the backhand return of service is usually weaker. Second, and even more important, is the nature of the American twist service, the favorite type of second serve. Its rapidly spinning ball naturally kicks high to the backhand and its medium pace gives the server maximum control and plenty of time to run well into the net position. In fact, American twist second serves hit deep to area 1 are just about equally as effective as fast first serves because the volleyer has time to get in closer to the net for his first volley. All young players should learn to master this simple yet most useful serve.

The important thing to stress on the second serve is to keep it deep. When the serve is deep you can win about 75 per cent of the points. But

Aim Points for Second Serves

The preferred aim points for second serves, numbered in order of preference, are recorded. The highly-favored American twist second service naturally spins the ball into the areas numbered 1 and 2 in each court. In the forehand court some 60 per cent of serves by the experts fall in these areas. About 15 per cent are sliced to area 3 to keep the receiver guessing, and the balance are scattered around. In the backhand court three fourths of all serves are aimed at areas 1 and 2, and the rest are split between area 3 and the rest of the court. The twist serve is employed so universally as a second serve because it provides three key advantages. First, it is easy to control, cutting down on double faults. Second, its slower speed gives the server enough time to get well into the net. And, third, its high-bounding kick to the backhand is one of the most difficult balls for the average receiver to return effectively.

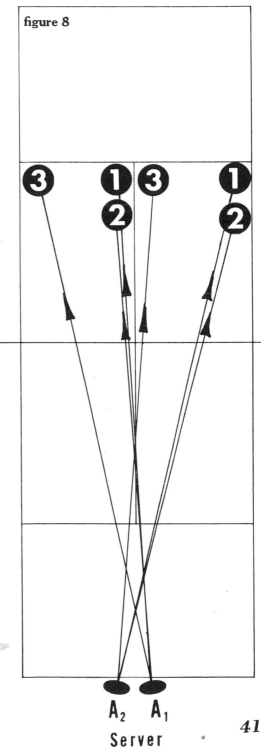

figure 8

A_2 A_1

Server

41

when it is shallow not even a Gonzales can win better than about 50 per cent of the points. Even the big time players get only half of their second serves deep, so that they are continually working to correct this defect.

Another way of emphasizing the importance of getting the first serve in play is to note the advantage it gives the server on his first volley. In fact, the first serve gives the server a better chance to put away the first volley by a vital three-to-two ratio over the second serve.

So much for the placing of the serve in connection with carrying out the first objective of the server—that of gaining the offense. The second and third objectives call for getting into the net position, and thinking and anticipating while so doing. On a fast court the modern game calls for following in behind *every* serve to the net position. (An amusing example of the importance of this was noticed in a match on grass between Gonzales and Hoad. Gonzales failed to follow serve in to net only twice in four sets. Each time he elected to remain on the base line he had a 40-0 lead, and was hoping to save a bit of energy. However, in both instances his hope backfired. He lost both points and had to come in to net at 40-15 each time to win the game.) The proper path to the net varies with the type and placement of the serve and the anticipated return of service. Examples of this will be explored more thoroughly under net play. At this moment it suffices to say that the server should swing his foot over the base line as he hits the service and sprint for the net. While doing so he must concentrate his attention not on the ball but on the receiver in order to anticipate the type, direction and speed of the return of service. We will pick him up at this exciting part of the point in chapter 6.

Slow Court Play

Data were collected on slow court play at the U. S. National Clay Court Championships.

Few players possess the ability to follow serve in to the net on a slow court. You will see exceptions from time to time when a serve and volley artist is up against a weak opponent. But when facing an adversary equipped with a good return of service, passing shots and lob, the net rusher will encounter real trouble. When a Gonzales cannot follow serve in to net on a slow court, as shown in Table VII, then *you* should think twice before trying to do so. This is not to say that occasional journeys to the net represent poor tactics. On the contrary, this procedure is recommended for the following reasons:

  1. To keep the opponent under pressure on his return of service by forcing him to watch you as well as the ball.

2. To prevent the receiver from hitting high, safe returns. By volleying away a few of these you can draw errors on the return of service as he will be compelled to keep the ball low.

The placing of the serve on the slow court is the same as that for a fast court with one exception. In serving to the forehand court most players prefer to place the first serve in the backhand corner (area 2, figure 7) about 50 per cent of the time, and use other parts of the court for surprise variants. The reason for this difference from fast court play is that you have more reason to try to draw a weak return from the backhand than to try to open up the court for a winning first volley.

There are two other items to remember. The first is to keep your serves deep. This usually prevents the receiver from making the deep or sharply-angled type of return which will steal the offensive away from the server. Data taken support this advice in that on deep serves the server wins points at a comfortable two-to-one ratio, while shallow serves result in a one-to-one standoff. The second is to get the first serve in as often as possible. This entails hitting the ball at somewhat less than maximum speed. The reasoning behind this suggestion is that the fast serve does not pay off on a slow court commensurate with the effort involved, while the good first serve usually keeps the receiver deep or on the defensive and saves the server valuable energy, as well as cutting down on double faults.

the Service Strokes

There are three principal types of service—the cannonball or flat service, the slice and the American twist—and the same basic rules of stance and delivery apply to each. Their variation lies in how the racket head strikes across or into the ball and in the follow-through to left or right. The service grip is the same as that used for the eastern backhand, with the racket handle held firmly but not too tightly.

More than any other stroke, the serve accents the importance of the left —or throwing—arm, since the shot cannot be hit properly unless the racket meets the ball at the top of the throw.

The fastest serve is not always the best, so it is wise to develop control first and to learn to mix up your delivery with changes of pace and spin. To get the slice service the ball is tossed so it is struck slightly to the right of the head with the racket following through across the body with your arm not quite fully extended. This imparts a rolling topspin to the ball

figure 9

Helen Wills Moody

The compiler of the greatest record in tennis, shown here wearing her familiar eye shade, demonstrates beautifully the American twist service. Note the great wrist snap action which has brought the racket across the ball from left to right. The stroke will finish back of the right foot as this foot comes over the line.

so that it bounces away from the opponent toward his forehand side. To get the flat service the ball is tossed not quite so far to the right and the ball is hit with a flat or open face with the follow-through ending on the left side. With the American twist serve the ball is tossed overhead and slightly to the left and the ball is hit with a snap of the wrist as the arm moves directly from left to right with the follow-through finishing on the right side (see figure 9). This imparts a spin to the ball so that it bounces high toward the opponent's backhand.

Actually the top servers learn to hit all three varieties of serves with essentially the same toss in order to avoid telegraphing to their opponent the type of service about to be delivered.

The service requires the coordination of two separate activities aimed at bringing the ball and racket into perfect union at the top of the swing (see figure 10). First, you should take a position within 4 or 5 feet of the center of the base line, allowing you to hit down the middle or angle the serve cross court. The left foot, pointing at a 45-degree angle toward the base line, should be 2 or 3 inches behind it to avoid the possibility of a foot fault, and the right foot about 18 inches behind the left. The weight is evenly distributed between the two. The racket is tilted upward at a slight angle, the throat cradled gently in the fingers of the left hand. The balls should be held comfortably in the fingers, not the palm. Relaxation and balance are the most important keys to the stance at this particular moment.

The stroke begins with both arms commencing their separate actions simultaneously.

The right arm moves down and back like a pendulum, the wrist remaining in a natural uncocked position until the racket is overhead and behind the back. When your elbow has reached the height of your shoulder in this continuous, circular backswing the wrist is broken and the racket head drops. There are variations in the length of the backswing. Some players (figure 11) arch the back and drop the racket head way down until it "scratches the back", while others (such as Talbert) have shortened the backswing. The important thing to remember is to have the shoulder, arm and racket in a pitcher's about-to-throw position before starting the forward motion. As the forward thrust begins, the wrist snaps the racket head forward, you achieve the feel of "throwing" the racket— just as if it were a baseball—across the net into the service court. The follow-through is natural with the weight shifting entirely to the left foot. Many players draw the right foot closer to the left foot just before hitting the ball. At impact the left knee is slightly bent. Once the ball is

figure 10

the Serve

At the start, racket is cradled in left hand, right elbow close, weight on back foot (1). Toss begins with racket backswing. Then start to shift weight forward as racket reaches bottom of swing (2). Body coil builds up power (3). As forward motion starts, the ball approaches peak (4).

2

1

3

4

figure 10

5

6

the Serve
(continued)

Toss must be accurate with body thrown forward, the ball met at full extension of racket and arm approximately 24 inches in front of the baseline (5). The left arm serves as a good counterbalance. Snap wrist forward, pointing the racket head toward the receiving court (6), shifting your weight to the left foot, which pivots only slightly throughout. Thereupon the right foot is pulled naturally forward, bringing the body back to anticipatory position (7 and 8).

7

8

figure 11

Richard A. (Pancho) Gonzales

One of the greatest of all servers is shown here at the end of the backswing with the racket head almost touching his back. Note the ball position and the body starting to lean forward so that all of his weight will be behind the delivery. Recently Gonzales has tended to shorten his backswing a bit.

struck, the right foot follows across the base line in the direction the ball is taking so that your weight is behind the shot and you are ready to start your sprint to the net or take the anticipatory position at the base line from which you are ready to begin the next stroke.

At the same time, the left hand has thrown the ball—in a natural, easy motion—to a point where the racket will meet it at the absolute top of the toss—the ball neither rising nor falling at the point of impact. The toss should leave the hand fairly high, with the left arm continuing up until it is fully extended, thus improving accuracy by limiting the distance the ball must travel to reach its peak. Intensive practice is required to achieve a correct toss, but it will pay off, as defective tosses, particularly low tosses, are responsible for many faults and poor serves.

If you find your serve is hitting the net or is too shallow, lift your sights by hitting "out" at the ball. And if your serves are going too deep, bring them back into the court by lessening the speed of the serve and increasing the spin on the ball. Spin lends control—even a server of the caliber of Pancho Gonzales seldom serves a truly flat ball in an entire match.

the Return of Service

There is no doubt that one of the most difficult strokes to execute both well and consistently is the return of service. Substantiation for this statement is not difficult when you consider that about 25 per cent of serves are not returned at all (see Table VIII), that service is broken only about one in five times and that the return of service enjoys a low potency (see Table VI). The vital importance of developing a reliable return of service is, therefore, obvious. This is the weapon with which service breaks are engineered. It is the stroke that sets the offensive and defensive tactics for each point.

The receiver should have in mind five major objectives:

1. Assume the most advantageous receiving position.
2. Anticipate the type of serve to be delivered.
3. Return the ball at all costs.
4. Force the server into making a defensive return.
5. Move in to the net at the earliest possible opportunity.

The reasoning behind these rules will become evident as this chapter unfolds. The logical way to begin is to analyze the starting position.

TABLE VIII

SERVES NOT RETURNED

Ranking Professionals And Amateurs

Surface	1st Serve	2nd Serve
Grass	35%	25%
Clay	25%	22%

The proper position for the receiver can be determined quite accurately by means of rather simple logic. Strangely enough, this logic is not well understood by many players, even those of the ranking variety. If you will just master the factors behind good position play, you will win a lot of points as a receiver. So, let's proceed to get these clearly in mind.

The best way to describe concisely receiver position play is by means of diagrams. The factors which the receiver must consider are the position of the server, the speed and spin of the service, the tactical situation and his own capabilities with respect to anticipation, speed and stroke production. These factors are explained briefly in figures 12, 13 and 14.

There has been a rather steady trend forward in the case of the position of the receiver. Back in 1886 Dr. James Dwight, father of American lawn tennis, stood well back of the base line to receive service. In the twenties Tilden was receiving at about 3 feet back of the base line. Borotra and Johnston stood on the base line. Then certain players such as R. Norris Williams and Henri Cochet began moving in until they were about 3 feet inside the base line. This development has been generally adopted as the soundest procedure by the top players of today. They move inside the base line as far as they dare, depending on the server. This is the proper counter to the serve and volley big game for the following reasons: (1) The earlier you return the service the sooner the server must hit his volley. (2) The earlier you hit the ball the easier it is to cover court, as the combined spin and speed of the serve have less opportunity to pull you wide of the court. In addition, you can make a better offensive stroke from the standpoint of both speed and angle from close in. (3) When the chance presents itself, it is easier for you to get in to the net as you are already a step or two on your way.

For many of these same reasons, and those covered in figures 12, 13 and 14, it is also recommended that the beginner and club player practice standing in to receive the serve and taking the ball on the rise. This is desirable whether playing on a fast or a slow court. In effect it gives you a better chance of taking the offense away from the server, whether he rushes the net or remains on the base line. This is, of course, especially true in the case of the second service. Anyone who has ever watched the amazing little Pancho Segura run in and around a twisting second serve off the racket of big Pancho Gonzales knows what we mean. He moves in to within 6 to 10 feet of the service line and powders the return of service with his forehand for many telling winners. This has a very upsetting effect on the server and teases him into double faulting. While you may not be a Segura, you are probably not facing the serve of Gonzales. So you can do the same at your own level of play, whatever that might be.

The major reason why a Segura can accomplish this is directly related to his ability to anticipate. The importance of this ability can hardly be overemphasized. You gain this tremendous advantage only by careful study of your opponent. A particular player is usually capable of serving better to the right or left. And most players telegraph the direction of the serve by the way they toss the ball and make the service stroke. For example, most players toss a bit to their right and in front for a slice serve, and swing across the body, toss straight and in front for a flat serve; and toss behind the head and swing away from the body along the base line for an American twist serve. Many have certain habits or favorite serves under certain tactical situations which further permit you to diagnose intentions. For these reasons you must study your opponent very carefully during his other matches, and during his warmups and play against you.

Lest you think this is poppycock, the matter of small, but giveaway habits is not unusual even among the tennis greats. Don Budge recently revealed to Bobby Riggs that he always knew, because of a certain mannerism, when Riggs was about to try for an ace. Riggs immediately indicated his disbelief. So Budge explained that ordinarily Riggs served with his racket head high and his wrist cocked upward, but when he wanted to serve hard, he lowered his wrist position in a telltale fashion which permitted Budge to get ready for a fast delivery. Riggs said, "I still don't believe it!" Quickly they found a racket to test the point. Just as Riggs started through the motions of a hard serve he turned toward a smiling Budge and cried out an incredulous, "Well, I'll be damned—you're right."

Of course another means of anticipation is to know your own weaknesses, as your opponent will almost certainly serve to take advantage of them in the majority of cases. For example, people usually served to the forehand of Frank Parker and Ken Rosewall and to the backhand of Frank Shields.

Now to return to the receiver's basic objective: that is, to get the ball back. The experienced player as well as the beginner should concentrate on achieving success in this department. After all, you can't win if you don't return the ball, and often even the saddest and feeblest of returns will draw an error from an overanxious opponent. In addition, by returning everything in sight you exert relentless pressure on the server. Many a server has become unsettled and has finally broken by being forced to win every point the hard way.

Position of Receiver

First Lesson — Direction of the Serve

Referring to the backhand court:

One objective of the receiver is to cover the court. In order to be able to reach serves hit to his right or left, he must be near the center of the area to which it is possible to direct serves. As a first step in determining proper position the receiver should note the point from which the server will make his delivery. He should then imagine a point M in the center of the service court, and take his position near the base line on a straight line drawn from the server through point M. For example, if the server stands at A_2, the receiver should stand near F_2, and if the server is at A_3, the receiver should move over to F_3. Some players stand a little to the right or left of the center line if they find their reach or stroke production is better from one side or the other.

Referring to the forehand court:

The straight, flat serve can be delivered only in the area defined by B_2 and B_3.

Therefore, the proper receiving position is, as just described, at the midpoint F_1. But this receiving position must be altered if the server imparts spin to the ball. A good slice serve curves to the right and can draw the receiver as much as 10 feet off the court to point B_4, and a twist serve can pull him to left a few feet to point B_1. Therefore, depending on the type of serve he faces, the receiver may be forced to modify his starting position to the right or left of the middle line A_1-M-F_1. In other words, you have to take a position midway between the limits of the *serving area capability* of the particular server opposing you. Thus, you might have to move your initial position from F_1 to midway point C. and be prepared to move to the right or left as you note from the server's toss the type of serve he is planning to deliver. This is why knowledge by the receiver of the server's capabilities and anticipation of the server's intentions is so important.

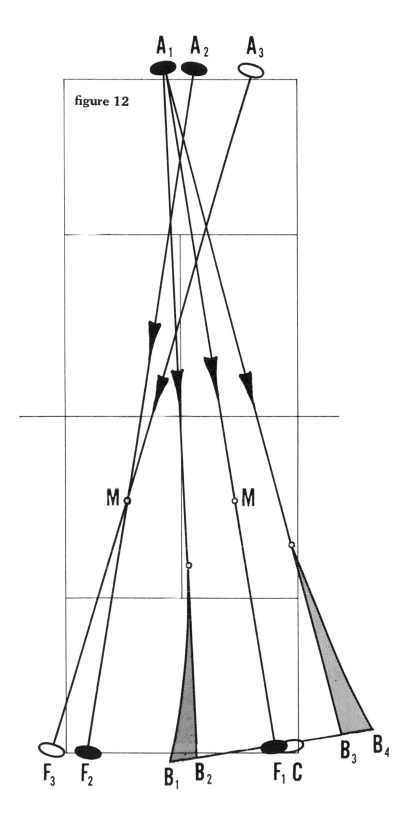

figure 12

Position of Receiver

Second Lesson — Speed of the Serve

The next thing the receiver must take into consideration is the speed of the serve. Since this becomes more important as the speed of the serve increases, let us take as an example to study a serve traveling at 90 miles per hour (the best ones exceed 100 mph). Such a serve travels the length of the tennis court in just six tenths of a second!

When you analyze carefully such factors as the speed and path of the ball, and the reaction time, speed and reach of the player, you find there is an area the receiver cannot cover (see shaded portion). This is true unless the receiver anticipates the intentions of the server and gets an explosive start in the proper direction. Note carefully that the deeper the receiver stands the *less* able he is to cover the rapidly widening and curving area open to the serve. Thus, modern players usually receive near B_1 rather than behind the base line at B_2 as did many of the old timers.

The closer in you stand along the line B_2-C, the better able you are to get your racket on the serve. But if you move in too close, you are faced with a more difficult shot because of the lower bounce on the ball. Thus, the general rule is to receive one to three feet inside the base line (B_1), or as far in as your style and talent permit against the server you are opposing.

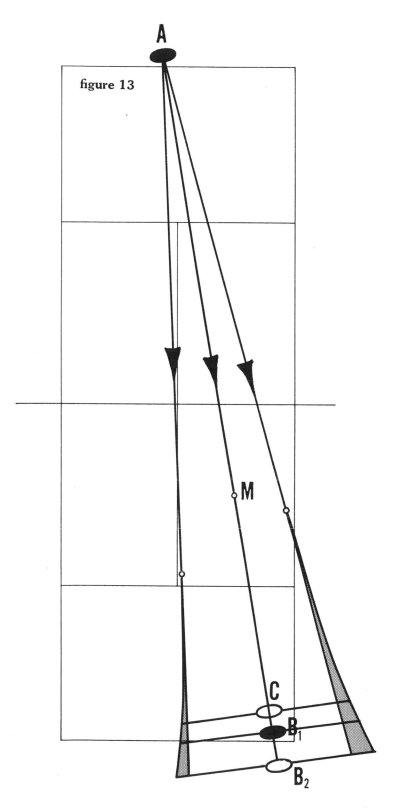

figure 13

Position of Receiver

Final Lesson — Tactics

Taking into account all factors, this figure shows the recommended positions for receiving first serves (forehand court) and second serves (backhand court). The areas are purposely left somewhat flexible, as the receiver must use his own good judgment to fit the particular situation.

The general conclusions drawn from figures 12 and 13 are to receive on a line bisecting the serving area capability, and as far inside the base line as possible consistent with good stroke production. Consideration of sound tactics for the receiver tends to fortify these conclusions.

Against a net-rushing server you gain a double advantage by standing as far forward as possible in area B₁. First you have a better chance of returning the ball at the vulnerable feet of the server, as you give him less time to run in to the net; and, second, you have a wider angle open for the passing shot by virtue of being closer to the net.

On the second service the receiver can take more chances and move in still closer in the B₂ area. This is because most second serves are of the slower American twist variety and tend to be more shallow as the server can ill afford the chance of a double fault. This will often allow you to take the offense away from the server by making a forcing return, and sometimes even permit you to take the net, particularly if the server stays back.

Finally, you have to keep working to determine just where to receive service to best advantage. This means you must develop your ability to anticipate the server's intentions; to learn how to take the ball on the rise; to make quick starts; to learn how to adjust your receiving position depending on your ability to move and reach to the right and left; and the relative strength of your forehand and backhand; and to know when to take chances or tease the server into errors. Remember in selecting receiving position that inches can make the difference between won and lost points.

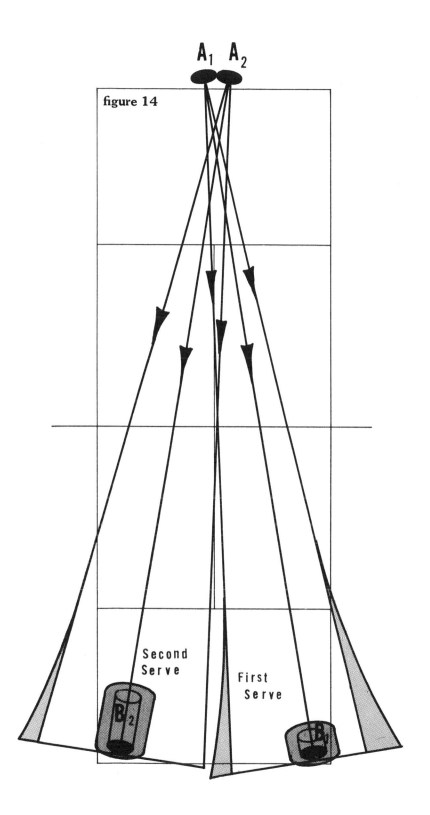

figure 14

A₁ A₂

Second
Serve

First
Serve

B₂

B₁

59

There is one fact about return of service that should be engraved indelibly upon the racket handle of every player as a constant reminder. Data taken on five hundred points in many matches indicate clearly that the receiver has almost an even chance of winning each point, once he has successfully returned the service. So, practice getting the return back consistently by any means possible—you will find it will pay off handsomely. To do so you must, above all else, keep your eye on the ball.

To give you a comparative measure so you can rate your performance, the top players return about seven out of ten first serves and second serves on fast courts. On slow courts they return about seven and a half out of ten first serves, and eight out of ten second serves. The better performance on the slow court is not due entirely to the slower, and truer, bounce. The receiver can usually play a safer return, higher and deeper, because the server is less likely to take the net.

Now it is time to turn our attention to the fourth objective of the receiver: that is, to force the server into making a defensive shot so the receiver can take command. The techniques to accomplish this will have to be considered in two parts—the shots to make, first, when the server rushes the net and, second, when the server remains on the base line.

There are two major points to keep in mind in returning serve against the player who follows serve in to net. These are:

(1) Take the ball as early as possible and keep the return low so that the server will not have time to get on top of the net, and will be forced to volley up defensively.

(2) Keep the server guessing by mixing up cross-court and down-the-line drives, dinks and occasional lobs. Avoid hitting to the middle.

The aim points used by the experts for return of service against the net rusher vary with the location from which the shot must be played. A great deal of information was collected on this subject during many tournament matches—on both grass and clay courts—involving the top players of the world. To provide some guide lines, let us take a look at figures 15, 16, 17 and 18.

Special attention should be given to figure 20, which summarizes the best aim points for returns of service against the net-rushing server.

Aim Points for Return of Deep Service Against Net-Rushing Server

On first and second serves hit deep to area 1 in the forehand court, the experts return some 40 per cent cross court to area 6, 40 per cent to the middle (area 7), and 20 per cent down the line to area 4 or 5. Most returns from deep serves are drives or slices with the dink used as a variant from time to time. As far as outright winners on the return are concerned, the cross-court and down-the-line shots hit from area 1 are about equally decisive. However, from area 3 the cross-court return to area 6 gives more outright winners. Most returns from area 2 are hit back to area 7. On the matter of over-all won and lost, the cross-court and down-the-line returns are almost equally effective—about 55 per cent of successful returns to these areas resulting in points won. Of returns to the middle (area 7), only 40 per cent result in points won.

This means that on deep serves to the forehand court the receiver should try to direct his return down-the-line or cross-court as shown in the diagram. Either one forces the advancing server to run further and reach for the volley, thus causing him to make errors, or weak volleys which present the receiver with opportunities to make successful passing shots. On the other hand, the return to the middle can usually be volleyed by the server less hurriedly and more effectively.

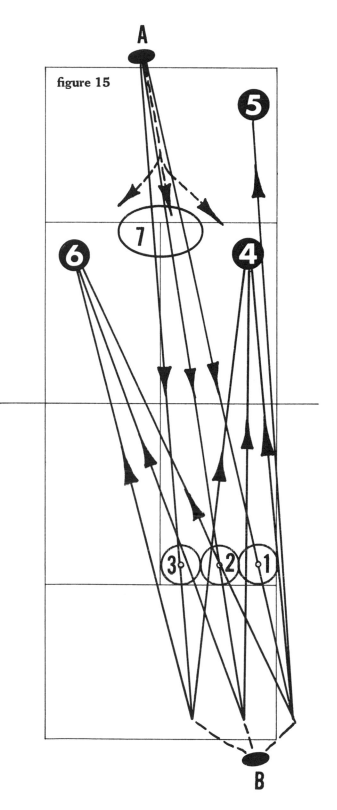

figure 15

Aim Points for Return of Shallow
Service Against Net-Rushing Server

On first and second serves hit shallow to the forehand court the experts favor the down-the-line return. Approximately 50 per cent of returns are hit down the line to areas 4 and 5, and 25 per cent each to areas 6 and 7. These returns are usually forehand drives or slices with an occasional dink mixed in.

Most outright winners are produced by down-the-line returns from area 1 and cross-court returns from area 3. On over-all won and lost, the down-the-line returns from areas 1 and 2 to areas 4 and 5 are certainly to be favored. From area 3 the cross-court return is more effective. These successful returns to the side lines win points in about 60 per cent of the cases. However, returns to the mid-dle (area 7) should be avoided as they lose more points than they win.

The receiver should learn to take advantage of a shallow serve by moving well in on the ball and hitting it crisply down the line, mixing in sufficient cross-court returns to keep the server guessing. Note the cross-court return can be more sharply angled when hit from a position closer to the net. Since these tactics will catch the net-rushing server back at a poor volleying position near the service line, the receiver should be able to win about two thirds of such points. But do not forget, you have to make the return. On sighting the opening, do not become overanxious and make an error.

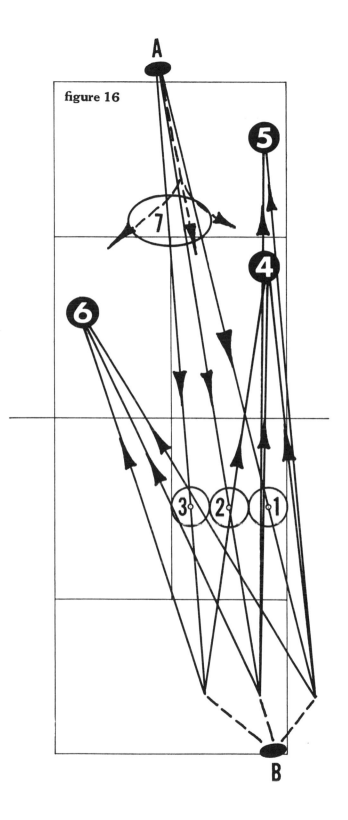

figure 16

Aim Points for Return of Deep Service
to Backhand Court Against Net-Rushing Server

On the first and second serves hit deep to the backhand court, the experts favor the cross-court return. Approximately 60 per cent are hit cross court to area 6, 25 per cent to the middle (area 7) and 15 per cent down the line to areas 4 and 5. The returns from deep serves are usually drives or slices with the dink used occasionally.

Most outright winners are produced by cross-court returns from areas 1 and 3, with some coming from down-the-line shots, particularly from area 1. On over-all won and lost, the cross-court and down-the-line returns are equally effective. Successful returns to these areas result in winning points in about 57 per cent of the cases. However, returns to the middle (area 7) win points only one time in three, so that this area is to be avoided.

Once again, this demonstrates that returns which force the server to run further and reach for the ball result in more errors and less decisive volleys. Obviously, this is the tactic for the smart receiver to follow.

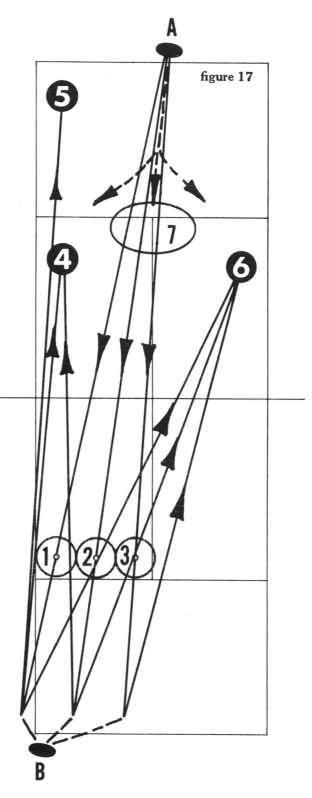

figure 17

Aim Points for Return of Shallow Service
to Backhand Court Against Net-Rushing Server

On first and second serves hit shallow to the backhand court the experts favor the cross-court return. Few serves ever land in area 3. Approximately 50 per cent of returns from areas 1 and 2 are hit cross court to area 6, 25 per cent down the line to areas 4 and 5, and 25 per cent to the middle area (area 7). In contrast to returns from shallow services from the forehand court, the majority of returns from shallow serves hit wide to the backhand court are sharply-angled dink shots. When the receiver gets in position fast enough to make the down-the-line return, it is usually a drive or slice.

Most outright winners are produced by the faster down-the-line return to areas 4 and 5. The pros often take the net behind a sharply-angled dink return from area 1 and try to put away the return volley (see figure 25). Returns to either side line result in winning points—about two thirds of the time. On the other hand, returns to the middle result in losing points about two thirds of the time.

The receiver should learn to take advantage of the shallow serve by moving forward into position rapidly in order to be able to take the ball early and drive or sharply angle it past the net-rushing server before he is past the vicinity of the service line. Such tactics should pay handsome returns.

figure 18

Composite Picture of the Best Areas for Return of Service Against Net-Rushing Server

This diagram is one which the receiver should stamp indelibly on his brain. It presents a summary picture of the best aim points for the return of service. This is the pattern which makes possible the engineering of the all-important service break.

The most lethal shots, which usually result in outright winners, are down-the-line or cross-court returns landing in the heavily-shaded areas. Note that the down-the-line and cross-court areas overlap somewhat. These heavier-shaded areas are recommended, as they force the volleyer to run far and to reach off balance as he strives to play the ball. Thus any return he is able to execute will usually leave him open to be passed on the succeeding shot.

The lighter-shaded portion in the middle, while much less lethal in producing outright winners, will often force an error or weak return if the serve can be taken early and the return made quickly enough to catch the server at the service line. Returns here at the feet of the volleyer make him volley up or attempt a difficult half volley.

Avoid the danger area whenever possible since this is the area in which the volleyer operates with greatest effectiveness—winning two out of three points. Returns to the shaded areas shift the odds in your favor—the receiver wins 60 per cent of points after returns of service to these areas.

Server

figure 19

Down the Line

At the Feet

Danger Area!

Cross Court

Down the Line

Cross Court

Receiver

Richard A. Gonzales

This return of service stroke by Pancho shows perfect form on the most-used return of service from the backhand court. He is caught in the act of hitting an underspin return from an American twist serve bounding high to the backhand. He has moved inside the base line to take the ball early and is about to draw the racket down and across the ball at an angle in order to hit a sharply-angled dink cross court. Gonzales plays this shot with a feathery touch which forces the net-rushing server to reach far and volley up.

figure 20

Return of Service When Server Remains on Base Line

Only a handful of players in the world have a sufficiently powerful service to permit them to play the big game and follow every service in to the net. And even these international experts can ill afford to do so when playing on slow courts. Therefore, the great majority of readers will ordinarily return service against an opponent standing near the middle of the base line. This calls for tactics and shots which are completely different from those just described. For this reason, it is imperative that the receiver develop the habit of noting first before executing his return whether the server is moving in to the net or remaining on the base line. Some types of returns which would be excellent against the base line player can be murdered if the server catches you off your guard and rushes the net, and likewise the reverse.

When the server remains back, the return of the serve must be kept deep—within 10 feet of the base line—to be effective. There is no sense in trying to keep the return so low that it is in danger of hitting the net —a mistake made by many weekend players. Instead, the shot should be played one or more feet above the net as a flat, topspin, chop or sliced drive. Even high, soft shots (half-lobs) which land near the base line are acceptable. The deep ball pins the server to the base line and often causes a shallow return which allows the receiver to take the offensive by hitting a forcing shot and taking the net. On the other hand, a shallow return, with few exceptions, hands the server the all-important advantage of taking the offense. To drive home the importance of this advice, remember the shallow return usually loses two out of three times, whereas the deep return gives the receiver a better than even chance of winning the point. The details of the proper aim points are shown in figure 21. Note the emphasis on returning service to the weaker backhand side.

If the server finds he is losing a lot of points as a result of high, deep returns, he will probably try an occasional trip to the net. Since such high returns are easy for him to volley, remember to watch him and be prepared to shift to the low, spinning return of service tactics shown in figures 15, 16, 17, 18 and 20. Such returns, you will find, are much easier to make from the slower, higher-bounding serve encountered on a slow court. Indeed, this is the reason even the best servers have trouble trying to rush the net on clay or composition courts.

Once the receiver has mastered the different types of returns of service against various servers, he will find he has a good chance to break service. But to do so, he must be ever alert to the changing tactics of the server.

Composite Picture of the Best Areas for Return of Service Against Server Remaining on Base Line

The best aim points for return of service are completely different when the server remains on the base line. This is the situation usually faced by most receivers the world over.

Above all keep the return deep—that is, within about 10 feet of the base line. If you just do that you should win at least 50 per cent of the points after such returns. While cross-court or down-the-line returns to the corner areas A and C are preferred in order to run the server, any deep return to areas A, B or C is acceptable, particularly in the darker-shaded portion near the base line.

If the serve is shallow, it is sometimes advantageous to hit a sharp cross-court return to area D or E. Such returns can result in outright winners or run the server so far off the court that his return can be put away.

By far the best tactic against most players without national ranking is to hammer away at the backhand by returning the great majority of serves to areas C and E. This takes advantage of the weaker side and sets the stage to outmaneuver the opponent.

By way of contrast, any returns of service to the danger area result in lost points about two out of every three times. A shallow shot in base line play usually opens up the flood gates in favor of the opponent. The drop shot should be used sparingly, and then only after faking a drive from a shallow service.

figure 21

Return of Service Strokes

The methods used in executing the forehand and backhand drives and the lob will be covered in Chapter 7—Base Line Play. As has been mentioned, these are among the accepted and valued methods of service return, and we do not wish to detract in any way from their importance by failure to describe them in this section. In fact, the major objective in service return is to get the ball back any way you can in order to capitalize on possible errors on the part of the server. If one type of service return stroke is not working for you, always have others in reserve to try.

The particular types of strokes to be described in this section are a family of shots which have come to be used specially for service returns against net-rushing servers. Most of these involve spin to develop control and to keep the ball low and slowly paced. This gives the volleyer three problems—he has to volley a spinning ball, he must volley up and the slow ball takes the sting out of his return. Meantime, the slow return gives you time to move into position for his shot.

The returns of the spinning type include the chop or chip, dink and slice. The chop is started with the racket head at about shoulder level with face open; the forward motion of the stroke is down under the ball to give it underspin (figure 22). The ball can be angled sharply or hit down the line by adjusting the position of the racket at moment of impact and the direction of the follow-through, which is shorter than for the drive. The slice is usually used to impart spin to a low ball. The racket actually slices under and across the ball from right to left on the forehand and left to right on the backhand, giving the ball a nasty sideways-bouncing motion. Dink is the term used for either type of spin shot when it is hit very softly, often at wide angles, just over the net. An excellent example of the start of such a shot off an American twist serve is shown in figure 19. All these shots are made easiest when the player utilizes the continental grip because of the flexible wrist action required in making the strokes.

figure 22

John A. (Jack) Kramer
A great champion and possessor of all the strokes in the book here demonstrates the chop return of service. Note the position of the wrist and short follow-through with racket face open to impart spin to the ball for accuracy and control. Played delicately, such returns force the net-rushing server to volley up.

chapter 6

Net
Play

There is no way more convincing to illustrate the revolution in top-flight tennis than to recall that as recently as 1928 the great Tilden was still winning matches without making a single volley. And calculating tacticians like Lacoste were just beginning to observe that "more and more the volley appears to be an indispensible stroke." Today the revolution is complete. In championship singles on fast courts hardly a point is played without at least one player camped at net in the volleying position. There is no doubt that the young player must now learn to be equally at home with the volley and overhead as with any other stroke.

This revolution is as sound as it is complete. The net position is the offensive position in tennis, and the volley and overhead are the knockout blows. The tactical pattern is to set the stage for a net stroke and then employ it for the kill. These contentions are borne out by the figures in Tables V, VI and VII, which show that the most lethal strokes as well as a high percentage of all winners are produced at the net, particularly on fast courts. The fact is that the top players punch or smash away from the net area one fourth to one third of all points won.

The aforementioned tactical requirement of setting the stage warrants emphasis. The volley might well be thought of as two consecutive strokes, the first involving an approach shot and the second the volley. For the volley to be a winner, the approach shot must be effective. The greatest weakness of many young players is a tendency to go to the net behind a serve or ground stroke which is insufficient to set the stage for a winning volley. This usually results in a lost point, as the opponent is presented with the opportunity to counter with passing shots. It is much like a boxing combination—you can seldom lead with the right; instead you have to set the opponent up by knocking him off balance with the left before you can rock him with your right. Practice to develop good forcing approach shots, which will drive the opponent off balance, is an essential part of the modern volleying game which is all too often overlooked.

Many weekend players seem to be afraid to venture into the net area. They do not feel at home up forward, nor do they appear to know what to do once there. Before this chapter is completed we hope we will have convinced the reader that net play is not only vital to the molding of a winning game, but also is easy to learn and adds a lot of fun to tennis.

Perhaps a simple example will help to show that the volley is not just a weapon for the expert with the big game, but is also of tremendous value to the average player or beginner. Figure 23 illustrates a type of point the reader will surely recall having played many times. It reveals clearly the value of using the volley for the kill.

Net play provides two major advantages. First, it allows you to capitalize on a good approach shot or a weak return. Second, it gives you the incalculable advantage of being on the attack with all the pressures upon the opponent which this involves.

To become a good net player it is necessary to learn the following: how to get to the net; proper volleying positions and anticipation of the opponent's return; proper placing of volleys and overheads; and the techniques of stroke production at the net. These factors will now be presented in this order.

How to Get to the Net

The player should go to the net only after he has prepared the way by means of a shot calculated to force a defensive return on the part of his opponent. There are essentially four types of approach shots which can provide the opportunity for moving into the net position:
1. A forcing serve.
2. A forcing return of service.
3. A forcing shot made from any shallow return, that is, from a ball bouncing more than 9 to 10 feet from your base line.
4. An offensive lob.

Many of the techniques of making these forcing strokes are described in chapters 4, 5 and 7. Here they will be tied more specifically into the manner of getting in to net behind them.

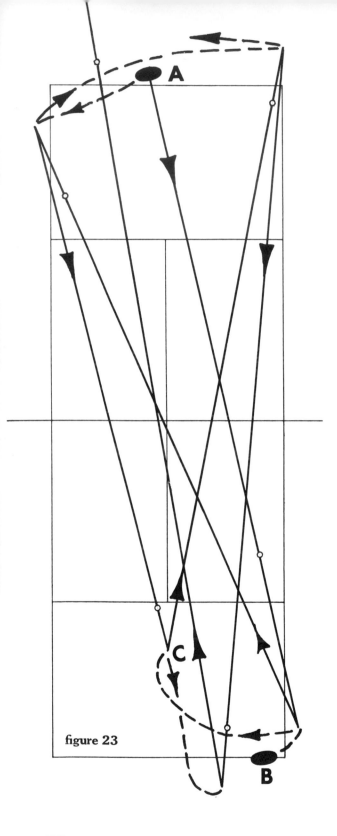

figure 23

the First Lesson in

These diagrams illustrate the wrong and the right way to play a point often encountered by the weekend player.

Server A is your arch rival whose service you are desperately trying to break on a hot July morning. In the left hand diagram you, receiver B, return the serve cross court and A returns a poor forehand to the middle. You seize the opportunity offered by running around the ball and hitting a fine forehand drive deep to the backhand corner. You have him at your mercy as he runs puffing to make a desperation shot with his weak backhand. But then you goofed by just standing entranced, hoping for an error. Somehow your rival managed to lunge at the ball and hit back a slow backhand which floated 6 feet over the net and landed near the base line,

the Value of Net Play

giving him plenty of time to get back into position. All of your hard-earned advantage was wiped out by one poor, feeble return, and you are forced to dash back to the base line to retrieve the ball. There, in trying too hard to recover the offense, you drive an off-balance forehand sailing over the base line to lose a point you once had in the palm of your hand.

The diagram on the right shows the same point as it should have ended. Having set the stage for the kill with the forcing shot to his backhand, you should have capitalized on the situation by moving into the attacking position at the net. From this position, you have the whole forehand court open for an easy volley placement before your rival can reverse direction.

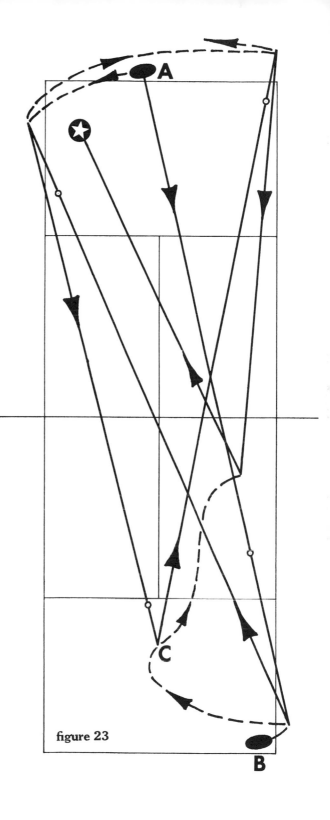

figure 23

On fast courts the present-day ranking tennis players always follow both first and second serves in to net. They have found by experience that rushing the net behind a powerful, deep serve will, in the majority of cases, set the stage for a winning point. From 10 to 23 per cent of the time the serve elicits an error on the part of the receiver, as he is forced to attempt to play a low, delicate return out of reach of the volleyer. And, in about 50 per cent of the cases, a successful return of service can be volleyed away for a win on the first or later volleys. First volleys account for about 17 per cent of all winners. Of the total points won, some 34 per cent are won at the net position.

On slow courts the serve, as we have already noted, is less potent. It accounts for some 3 to 18 per cent of points and provides a safe journey to the net only 15 to 20 per cent of the time, even among experts. First volleys are far less effective and account for only 2 to 14 per cent of the winners. Subsequent net strokes bring the total number of winners at net to to some 25 per cent.

For a serve to be sufficiently forcing to provide you with a good chance to make a telling first volley, it must be hit deep. Against most players the deep serve should be to the backhand side as the return will ordinarily be weaker and, therefore, easier to volley. The only acceptable shallow serve is one so sharply angled to the forehand or backhand courts that it causes the receiver to move considerably beyond the side line to reach the ball.

To impress upon you the importance of this, remember, as stated in chapter 4, that deep serves allow you to win two out of three points. Even if you lack a powerful serve, it is wise to follow it to net on occasion in order to rattle the receiver. When, on any given point, you do decide to hit your deep serve and go in, the speed and direction of your approach run are both vital. You have to get your foot over the base line as you hit the serve and really sprint for the net. Getting halfway to net is murder—if you cannot get way in so as to avoid difficult half volleys, you'd better stay back. The best volleyers run in fast four or five steps and, as they reach the area just behind the service line, bring the feet into the same line and make a hop with the weight equally balanced on both feet. (This is why you can see a worn area near the service line after a few matches on a grass court.) While so doing they anticipate or see the direction of the return and then continue their forward motion to intercept the ball as close to the net as possible. Of course, in the case of a lob, they would reverse direction and prepare to hit an over-head. The best path to the net depends on the bounce point of the serve. The principle to remember is that you should run to the net nearly along the bisector of the angle of possible returns, arriving at the volleying position with weight well balanced. You should favor the down-the-line side of the bisector because the faster return can be made on that side. This is explained simply by means of diagrams as shown in figure 24. Note carefully how important it is to be as close to the net as possible (6 to 9 feet) and positioned laterally within a matter of inches from the point which gives you best court coverage. Remember that from most parts of the court the receiver has room to pass you on either side. If you are a step out of position or arrive off balance, the receiver is presented with a relatively simple passing shot.

There are other things which are helpful to keep in mind when going to net behind a serve. Most opponents have certain habits which, when diagnosed, will provide you with an advantage in getting to the proper volleying position. A review of figures 15 and 18 on returns of serve will assist by providing such helpful hints as:

a. Most deep serves are returned cross court. This is particularly true for serves to the backhand court, especially the forehand corner. The smart server should favor the cross-court side of his proper approach path just a bit if he finds his opponent follows this standard pattern for returns.

b. Shallow serves to the forehand court are usually returned down the line. This means the server should be prepared to protect this area as he moves in to net.

c. Shallow serves to the backhand court are returned cross court in the majority of cases. The server must be aware of this if he is to have a chance of successfully volleying such returns.

d. While the server is well-advised to play these percentages, in doing so he should try to note any giveaway motions by the receiver which will indicate either a cross-court or down-the-line return. The reason this is so important is that returns to either side are by far the most difficult for the net-rushing server to handle, as he must extend his reach to the maximum in order to meet the ball thus returned.

81

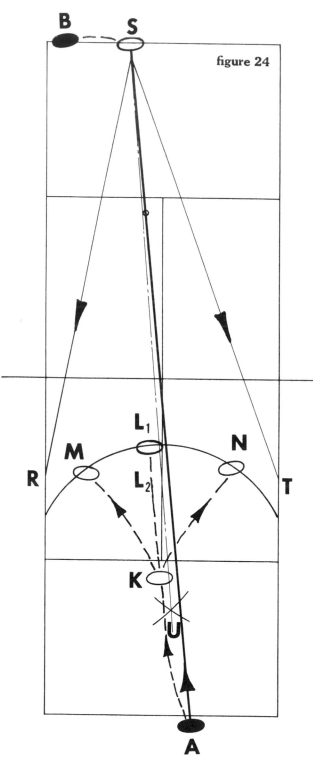

figure 24

Going to Net

On the left is depicted the simplest case when the serve is to the middle. The possible angle of return is RST and the bisector of this angle is SU. The best path to the net is just a few inches on the down-the-line side of SU since a slightly faster return can be hit down that side. As the server runs in he pauses momentarily for his balanced hop at point K, after which he will move normally toward point L_1 or some other point such as M or N, depending on the direction of the return of service. Note that for every foot closer to the net along the L_2 to L_1 line, the server gains by having about 1 foot less width of court to cover. A driven return off a fast service seldom gives the server enough time to get in much closer than a step inside the service line. However, the server has a chance to cover such shots, because a hard drive cannot be hit at a wide angle along lines SR and ST, as it will sail over the side line.

On the right is shown the proper approach following a serve wide to the backhand corner. From point E receiver B has a wider effective angle of return, DEF. The reason for this is, in large measure, the speed of the return. Whereas, just as in the case of the lefthand diagram, any angled return along line ED must be hit delicately, the long down-the-line shot to point F can be hit with blistering speed. This means that a server standing along the bisector G would have an easy time protecting the left

Behind Serve

side, but would be wide-open for a fast passing shot down the line. To compensate for this and gain best command of the net the server must approach the net on a line about 3 feet on the down-the-line side of the bisector to point L. Notice once again the advantage proximity to the net provides by decreasing the width of territory the volleyer must cover. The limit of the volleyer's forward advance is set by the ability of the opponent to lob effectively.

These diagrams also serve to illustrate the difference between the so-called center theory and the corner theory. On the left the advance to the net is from a bill hit to the center. This has the advantage of giving the opponent the smallest angle for a passing shot, but has the disadvantage of letting him make his return, often with his forehand, from a spot where he is in perfect position to await your next volley. On the right the angle serve to the backhand gives the opponent a wider angle of return for a passing shot, but the volleyer has offsetting advantages. His approach shot forces the opponent to run and reach for the ball while trying to execute a passing shot from his weaker backhand side. And the court is open for a winning volley down the other side.

Knowing the correct position to take at the net against your opponent is an invaluable asset. Inches often make the difference between making your volley effectively or being passed or forced to err.

figure 24

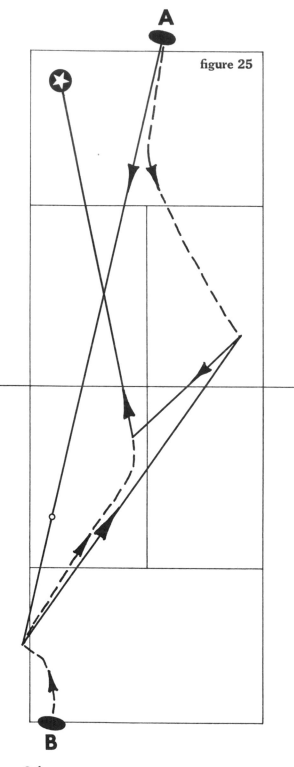

figure 25

Going to Net Behind

It is not often that a receiver gets an opportunity to go to net on a return of serve. Such openings occur only when the serve is shallow, as shown in this figure.

On the left is the classical approach against the net-rushing server. This is the exception to the rule that approach shots must be hit deep. Receiver B moves way in on a shallow second serve and plays a sharply-angled cross-court dink to force the server to volley or half-volley up from close to the net. Knowing that just about the only shot server A can play is cross court over the low part of the net, receiver B moves in toward the middle

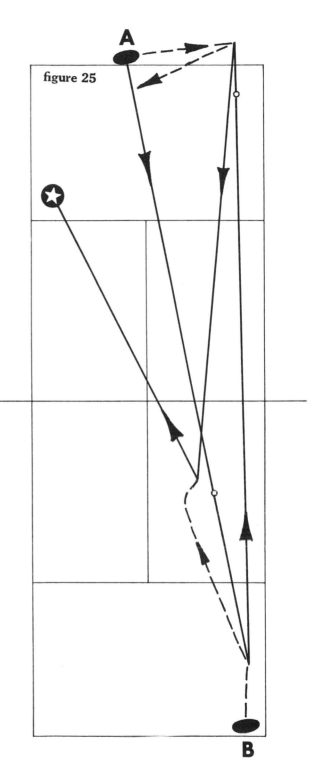

figure 25

Return of Service

volleying position as shown.
His perfect tactics permit him
to volley the return for an easy
placement.

On the right is shown the
proper approach shot when
the server, A, does not come in
behind a shallow serve. Receiver B moves rapidly to
take the ball on the rise and
plays it deep down the line.
He continues moving forward
to the net position and is rewarded for his action with an
easy volley for the point.

These two patterns are re-
peated often, whenever the
server is guilty of serving
badly, whether the court is
fast or slow.

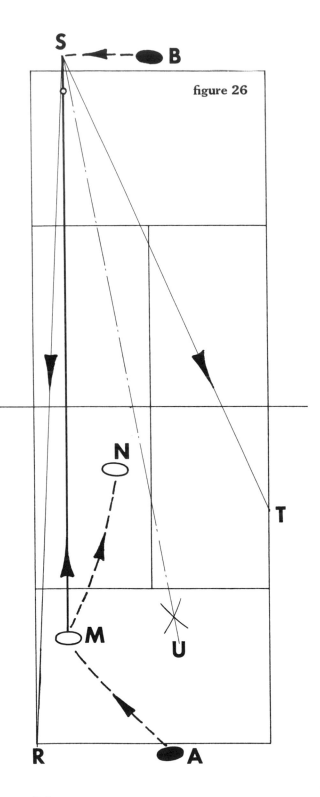

figure 26

Going to Net Behind

These figures illustrate two methods of getting to the net after a shallow return to point M. On the left is the manner which the top players usually employ. They hit down the line deep and move in to the net to point N on the down-the-line side of the bisector SU of the possible angle of return RST. Note that the distance player A has to run to get to the proper net position is a minimum.

On the right is the method often used by weekend play-

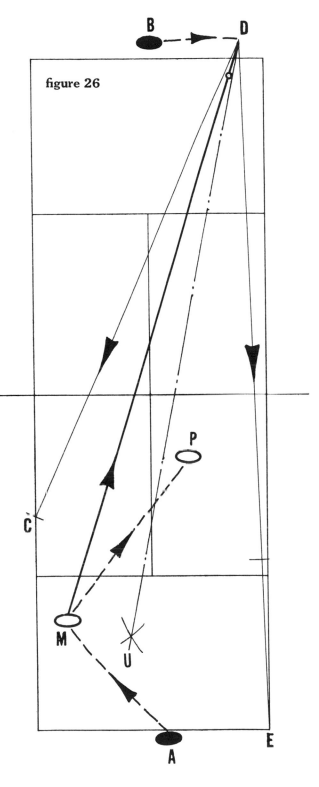

figure 26

a Ground Stroke

ers. They choose the crosscourt return deep to the backhand in order to take advantage of the fact that they expect a poor return from the backhand side of most opponents. But note in this case how much further (4 to 5 feet) player A has to run to reach the proper volley position at point P. An expert would have much more time to whip a passing shot down the line along DE, which is the very reason the top players usually avoid this tactic.

In going to net behind other shots, such as return of service, ground strokes or offensive lobs, many of the principles enunciated for the serve apply. The approach shot must be hit deep in the great majority of cases in order to be effective. Deep forcing shots are easier to make from a weak, shallow shot, whether a serve, volley or ground stroke. Also it is much easier to get to the net if you start your run from a point already part-way there. Some 90 per cent of such journeys to the net begin by taking advantage of a weak, shallow shot landing more than 10 feet from your base line. To attempt to go in from deeper in the court is too risky. The forcing shot favored is deep to the backhand corner. This is not only because it is the weaker side, but also because a lob return usually permits a good chance at a forehand overhead, whereas a lob from the forehand corner may have to be hit with a difficult backhand overhead. There are, of course, exceptions. The professionals almost invariably hit the forcing shot down the line because this maneuver provides the shortest path to the proper volleying position. They reserve the cross-court approach shot for cases when the opponent is out of position. Among lesser players the cross-court approach hit deep to the backhand is used much more often because the return will usually be weaker from that side. Various methods of getting to the net are shown in figures 25 and 26.

The ground stroke approach shots are among the most beautiful in tennis. No one who ever saw Kramer or Perry go in to net behind a running forehand drive can forget the picture of balance, timing, rhythm, power and speed. The whole operation of moving to the ball, stroking it and running to the net appeared to be one fluid, devastating motion.

Proper Volleying Positions and Anticipation

The proper volleying position at net is that point on the court which gives you the best chance of playing offensively your opponent's return. To volley offensively it is best to be close to the net in order to hit down on the ball. But you cannot move in too close, lest you be lobbed. The best compromise is to stand 6 to 9 feet from the net, depending in part on your height and agility. This means that the proper volleying position for most cases is in the center of the court astride the line that divides the service courts at a point 6 to 9 feet from the net. We will refer to this as the basic volleying position.

But you must not assume that once you have reached the basic volleying position you can afford to remain glued to the spot. It is possible for an opponent to pass you from almost any point on the court, so your objective is to be sure you can get your racket solidly on the ball. This entails shifting your net position according to your opponent's position and the type of stroke he is about to make. Unless you can anticipate the direction and type of passing shot, you stand to lose the point.

Adjustment of net position to take into account the opponent's position has already been mentioned in the preceding section. A further description of the factors to consider is given in figure 27.

Anticipation is an art and, as with all arts, you have to spend time developing and sharpening your talents. To anticipate you must violate one of the cardinal rules of tennis — you have to take your eye off the ball.

To begin at the beginning, there are four steps in anticipation. The first step in anticipation starts with your own shot. As a result of placing the ball in a particular spot and knowing your own position and that of your opponent, you should have a good idea what the return is likely to be.

The second step is to gather some intelligence data on the opponent. Most players have favorite shots, habits or motions which give away the type of shot they are about to make. The style and method of stroke production employed often provide important hints. Time spent in studying your opponent in his earlier round matches will pay off handsomely. For example, a player with topspin is more liable to pass cross court than one who uses a flat drive. Often you will note that a player may fool a good opponent once by some trick shot, but the second time he tries the same thing it will backfire. This is because the good player has noted some giveaway motion which he carefully files in his memory and uses to spot the same shot whenever it is next employed.

The third step is that of concentrating on the position and motions of the opponent as he prepares to strike the ball. In accomplishing this you have to take your eye off the ball and watch the over-all actions of the opponent. This means noting the position of his body, feet, arms, backswing and racket. They telegraph the motion of the racket and the angle and speed with which it will contact the ball. This then permits you to predict the direction, speed and spin of the shot so that you can move to the proper place and be prepared to make the return. While it may seem difficult to take all of these signs into account in one quick glance, you will find it is actually fairly easy to learn with some practice and experience. For example, it soon becomes obvious that a ground stroke will be hit cross court if the ball is struck a bit in front of the player with a racket motion from the side lines toward the center of the court, and down the line if the ball is struck a bit late with a straight through motion (see figure 28).

figure 27

The first step in anticipation is to know the situation. Here are two typical points where this knowledge is vital.

The lefthand diagram is a simple example of anticipation. Server A has run receiver B off the court a bit with a slice serve and then volleyed the return of service cross court to the open area. However, the volley lacked pace, and server A notes that the opponent can reach the ball after a long run. So he has to decide how best to cover the net. If you are server A, you should watch your opponent, not the ball. You will note that he is running diagonally away from the net and reaching with arm extended to play the ball slightly behind his body, while swinging down the line. With such a swing from this position he cannot hit cross court, but will have to play down the line into the cross-hatched area (R) with a drive, low slice or lob. Therefore, your next step is to move toward point D to be in proper position while continuing to diagnose which type of shot will be played. From point D you obviously have only a short distance to move to cover any type of return and play a forehand volley or overhead cross court to area 1 for the point. On the other hand, if you had remained near the center of the court at point E, a desperation drive down the line by receiver B might well

Anticipation

have stolen what should have been an easy point.

On the right is shown a tougher problem. As server A, you are forced to make a difficult first volley at point L, and succeed only in making a shallow, low-bouncing volley to point R. This puts you in real trouble, and quick thinking is imperative. First you should decide that it is unlikely that receiver B will try to lob a low ball. This means you should stay close to the net to minimize the area you must protect against his passing attempt. The whole left side of your court is open for a passing shot to area S. But if you start running too soon to cover the logical return to this area, receiver B will change his shot and chip one down the line to area T. The best solution is to move back to point M between the two areas and pause there a moment, being careful to maintain proper weight balance so that you can move in either direction. While poised, you must take your eye off the ball and study your opponent for a fleeting instant. Here is where knowledge of his style is priceless. Having diagnosed the side down which the opponent appears committed to try to pass you, you then proceed to scramble for the shot with throttle wide-open and eyes glued on the ball. Sometimes a brief prayer helps at this point.

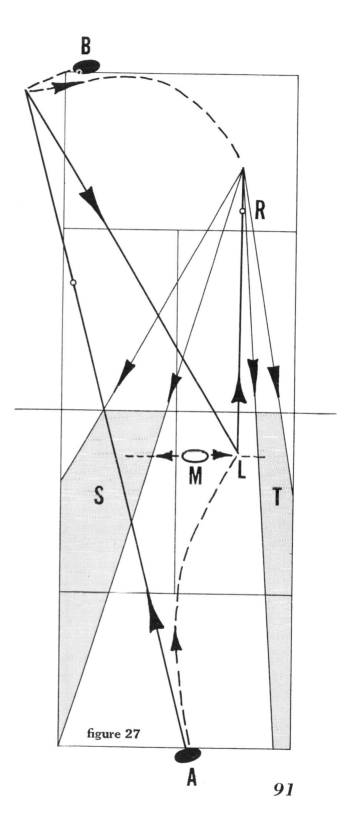

figure 27

The fourth and final step in anticipation is to learn how to take maximum advantage of your knowledge. Half of the art of anticipation is to hide the fact that you have anticipated your opponent's shot until just the proper split second. If you move too soon to intercept the shot, your opponent will cross you up by changing direction, and if you wait too long, the ball will pass you. You must learn to time your move with great accuracy. Then finally, you should shift your attention from the opponent to the ball and fix your eyes firmly upon it until you have executed your stroke and are ready to start the anticipation sequence once again. The first move is to get back into position—normally, the basic volleying position.

The ability of the experienced player to anticipate the opponent's intentions is truly remarkable. We attended a long match between Gonzales and Hoad once just to collect information on this point. To our amazement, only twice during the entire contest did these two great players get caught on the wrong foot! In other words, they were essentially always moving in the right direction to meet the ball and were never embarrassed by zigging when they should have zagged, as often happens among weekend players. To accomplish this feat certainly requires a superb sense of balance and a perfect grasp of the four essential steps in anticipation. A few selected points shown in figures 28 and 29 illustrate anticipation in action.

It behooves the player who is trying to improve to learn also how to counter the anticipatory powers of an opponent. The way to do this is to fake shots from time to time and to develop the habit of starting all your strokes with nearly the same motion. This will tend to confuse your opponent and to hide your intentions until it is too late.

Proper Placing of Volleys and Overheads

Once you attain the net, the experts all agree, you have to go for the kill. If you cannot and are forced to play a defensive volley, by all means hit the ball deep. Just remembering and carrying out these two commandments will go a long way toward making your net play effective.

In championship tennis on fast courts, once the serve and return of serve are executed, three out of every four points are won at net. The importance of developing a decisive volley is, therefore, obvious. Just to poop the ball back gives the opponent an open invitation to pass you on the next shot. The better players, except in rare instances, hit uncompromisingly for the opening and the point.

The most important volley during a point is the first volley since it sets the stage for the ultimate outcome of the point. In today's tennis the first volley is usually made off the return of service. The first volley is not only the most important, it is also the most difficult volley to make because of the long run required to reach the ball. This means that it is essential to have a clear understanding of the tactics which should be employed. Therefore, in order to evolve a sound basis for tactical instruction, hundreds of first volley points involving numerous top-flight players were recorded and studied. From this emerged a clear pattern which should be mastered by beginner and expert alike. A summary diagram showing the positions from which first volleys should be made and the areas into which they should be hit is given in figure 30. It is difficult to overemphasize the importance to the singles player of having this over-all picture of first volley tactics clearly stamped in his memory. Once this is accomplished, it is easy to proceed beyond to the understanding of individual point situations.

When making the first or subsequent volleys, sound tactics, it must be remembered, also involve going for the kill. This generally means hitting the ball where the other fellow isn't. There are a number of types of openings for volley placements such as:

1. A wide-open court, created by a great approach shot, which provides an opportunity where almost any kind of volley can win, even if stroked by your ailing grandmother.

2. A small opening into which you must volley with great speed in order to beat your opponent.

3. A small opening into which you must play a low bouncing ball just out of reach of the opponent by executing a soft or spinning volley.

4. A surprise opening which you obtain by catching the opponent moving in one direction and punching your volley neatly behind him. Often one false step on his part is all you need for such openings.

5. A created opening which you accomplish by deliberately faking one type of volley and then changing direction or speed at the last moment in order to fool your opponent. This is particularly effective when one fakes the deep volley and hits a deft stop volley.

When in doubt or when none of these five opportunities for a volley placement occurs, you should volley deep, usually to the backhand. But the most important thing is to keep the ball deep, as the opponent will have much less chance to pass you with his return. This is especially true if you are forced to reach wide and hit a defensive volley — here the deep

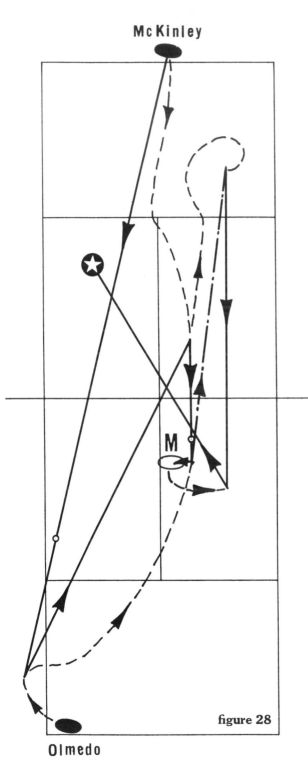

McKinley

M

figure 28

Olmedo

Anticipation

These two points were taken from a match between two fast players, Alex Olmedo and Chuck McKinley, during the 1959 U. S. National Championship at Forest Hills.

On the left server McKinley attempts a drop volley as his first volley. However, it is anticipated by Olmedo who plays a lob return. This shot McKinley anticipates in time to move back quickly and get set for an overhead and, presumably, an easy point. But "the Chief" is not to be denied. He moves quickly to his left to attract the attention of McKinley and pauses at M as he sees McKinley set himself a bit early for an overhead down the line. Then he sprints for the side lines and makes a miraculous cross-court volley from the overhead smash for the point as his opponent gasps in amazement.

On the right it is Olmedo's turn to be amazed. The point begins with Olmedo, the serv-

in Action

er, playing a short volley. Mc-
Kinley tries to pass him cross
court, but Olmedo anticipates
and plays a drop volley. But
McKinley sees this coming
and lobs well over Olmedo to
the base line. This is retrieved
by Olmedo and returned with
a drive to the middle on
which McKinley tries to fool
him with a drop volley. However, "the Chief" sees this immediately and roars in to take
advantage of a perfect passing
opportunity. In this delicate
situation McKinley concentrates with every fiber to diagnose Olmedo's next move. By
good fortune he sees that Olmedo's feet and backswing
telegraph an angle shot to his
backhand. He decides to
pause just long enough at N
so that Olmedo cannot change
direction, and then dives to
his left. His resulting cross-
court volley for the point
brought forth well-deserved
cheers from the gallery.

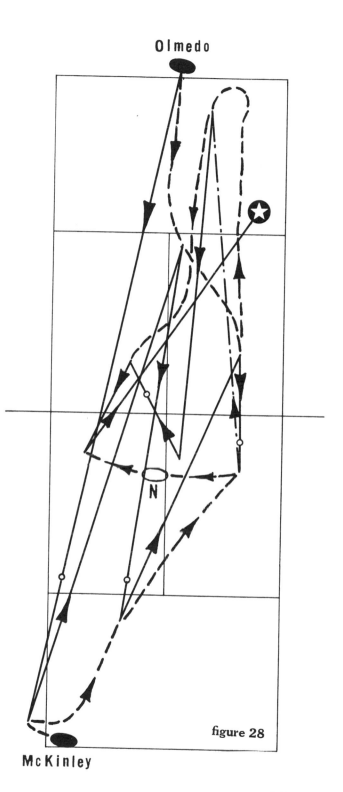

Olmedo

N

McKinley

figure 28

MacKay

figure 29

Fraser

Great

These are two points played by Neale Fraser in the 1959 Davis Cup Challenge Round which illustrate his great ability to anticipate.

On the left his serve is returned beautifully down the line so that he is barely able to half-volley rather feebly cross court, presenting Barry Mac-Kay with an easy passing opportunity. In this desperate situation Fraser starts back toward the middle of the net while keeping a careful eye on MacKay (not the ball), and slowing his momentum so that he can reverse direction if necessary. The split second he sees that MacKay is committed to try to pass by hitting cross court behind him, he reverses and lunges for the ball to pull off a great saving

Anticipation

volley for the point.

On the right Fraser, as receiver B, returns the ball at MacKay's feet, forcing him to play a weak volley. Fraser tries to chip a passing shot down the line but MacKay anticipates this and moves over to volley. Again Fraser watches MacKay rather than the ball and notes that he is about to volley the ball in front of his body with his racket moving from side line toward the center — positive proof the shot will be cross court. So Fraser, now at point M, turns his attention back to the ball and to pouring on the speed. As a result, he is able to just reach the ball and to execute a fine volley down the line to win the point.

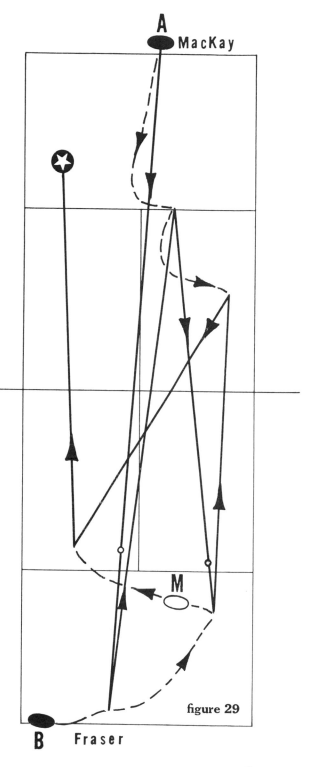

figure 29

This diagram warrants careful study, as it contains a world of information on the first volley. Data taken from many matches provide the basis for valuable instruction on proper areas from which to make the first volley, and where the volley should be placed. With this understanding of what happens on the average, it will be easy to develop the habit of making the proper move during individual points.

The over-all objective of the server in making his first volley is to place the ball out of reach of the receiver or to force him to play a defensive return. This means the server must volley the ball outside the central Danger Area—when he does so he will win eight out of ten points. On the other hand, if he volleys into the Danger Area he gives the receiver plenty of time to reach the ball and an excellent passing shot opportunity — in fact, the server will win only four out of ten points.

The lower part of the figure shows first volley positions. The most important thing to remember is that the server should get in as close· to the net as possible by moving in to area D or C. (He should have time to reverse himself if he anticipates lobs properly.) If the server is slow and gets caught in area A, he will be in serious trouble. First, he is liable to make an error or be passed, particularly if the ball is near either side line. (Refer to figure 20 on Return of Service.) And even if the server does make the volley he will lose six out of ten points, as he will hit many shots up weakly and place about one third of them in the Danger Area. Getting to area B offers little improvement. From here the server will win only about half the volleys he makes, as he is pulled way out of position and will again hit about one third into the Danger Area. However, if the server gets in far enough to cut off the return of service and volley from within area C, the odds turn heavily in his favor. He should win seven out of ten times and volley not over 30 per cent into the Danger Area. From area D the server is able to hit down at an angle, drop-volley or hit deep at will, placing only one in five in the Danger Area and winning nine out of ten points. A little more than half the volleys should be made from area C and about 10 to 15 per cent each from areas D and B. The remaining 25 per cent from area A are forced upon the server usually because he has delivered a shallow second serve or is slow in moving to net.

The upper part of the figure shows the proper aim points for first volleys. The necessity of avoiding the Danger Area

for the First Volley
to the Forehand Court

has already been noted. The most important thing to learn is that if the server will just keep his first volley deep (in the speckled area within 10 feet of the base line), he will rarely lose. From deep it is almost impossible for the receiver to pass an alert net player. On grass the favorite tactic of the experts in serving to the forehand court is to serve wide to pull the receiver off the court and then volley deep to area R in the opposite corner. This maneuver keeps the ball out of reach of the opponent and wins nine out of ten times. Shots are aimed effectively at the drop or stop volley areas only when volleying from up forward in area C or D. Angle volleys are also most effective when made from well up in the court. Note that the safe area T for angle volleys is longer and wider on the backhand side when serving to the forehand court. The selection of just which volley to make depends on the relative positions and movements of the players. When in doubt as to the proper volley, it is best to volley deep, as this puts the receiver on the defensive and gives the server time to move to the best position for his second volley.

The diagram for serves to the backhand court is just the same except that the angle volley area T and the deep volley area R are reversed.

Receiver

figure 30

Server

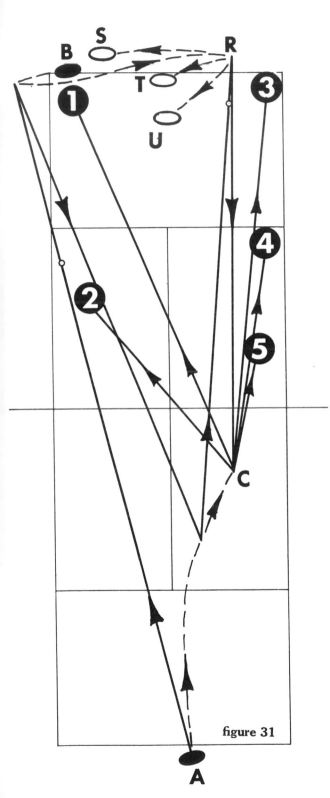

Placing

These diagrams illustrate some of the techniques necessary in going for the kill with the volley. The object is to hit the ball out of reach of the opponent. This means hitting to an open space or catching the opponent moving one way and then hitting behind him.

On the left is shown a case where several choices are open to the volleyer; the purpose of the figure is to point out the importance of making the proper choice. Receiver B has returned server A's first volley down the line, and server A is getting set to make his second volley from point C. In a brief moment server A must decide where to place his volley. Let us examine his problem as he notes the location and the direction and speed of movement of his opponent.

If receiver B hesitates too long at point R, it is best for the server to volley cross court to aim point 1 or 2. If hit from below the level of the net, the ball should be volleyed deep to area 1, and a high ball should be angled more sharply to area 2.

If receiver B hesitates at R and then commits himself by running hard toward point S, the volley should be hit behind him, as he will be unable to reverse direction. A high ball can be hit severely to area 3; a ball hit from below the net can be sent spinning low

figure 31

the Volley

to area 4 or drop-volleyed to area 5.

If receiver B moves to point T and is poised to move in any direction, server A must select the best shot based on the height of the ball. Often it is best to fake one way and volley another. When in doubt, the server should volley deep.

If receiver B suspects a short volley and moves in to point U, the volley should be hit deep behind him to area 3.

On the right is shown what happens when each volley just misses in decisiveness against a determined defender.

Hoad, the server, angles the first volley, but not enough to prevent Gonzales, the receiver, from reaching the ball and trying to chip a passing shot down the line. Hoad anticipates this and angle-volleys cross court to open country. But again it is not sufficiently sharp, and Gonzales is able to reach the ball after a hard run. He tries to fool Hoad by a cross-court return, but Hoad again anticipates and hits a third volley angled slightly toward the side line for what he thought was an easy winner. But he has failed to put enough pace on the ball and Gonzales, after a desperate sprint, makes an amazing backhand passing shot down the line for a well-deserved win. This represents scrambling at its best.

A Hoad

figure 31

Gonzales   **B**

volley gives you time to get back into position. Such volleys should be hit down the line as flicked cross-court attempts will result in too many errors.

Some of the aspects of placing the volley are illustrated in figure 31.

Much the same thing can be said about the placing of ground strokes hit from inside the service line. You should go for the kill whenever possible. When in doubt, the best practice is to hit deep down the line.

The overhead is the most lethal stroke in tennis. The general rule is to hit all out for the kill whenever you are closer to the net than a point about 5 feet from behind the service line. From further back the ball should be blocked back deep in order to keep the opponent pinned to the base line, and to give the striker time to get back in to the net position.

The overhead is usually placed deep in one corner or the other if hit from the neighborhood of the service line. From closer in it is best to angle the overhead to open country for an almost certain point. It is important to remember two additional things. Overhead errors are 75 per cent netted and only 25 per cent outs. So hit them deep, hard and accurately.

When selecting the spot to aim the overhead, it is necessary to glance at the opponent just before you stroke the ball in order to see which way he is committed to move. It is most embarrassing to forget this important detail. Every player cringes at the memory of a lost point he had already counted as won after smashing a tremendous overhead, only to look up and find the opponent there waiting with a diabolical grin on his face and a perfect passing shot coming off his racket. A celebrated case of this sort happened once to unsettle the great Von Cramm at Forest Hills. Playing on the end court of three, he smashed a savage, angled overhead against Bitsy Grant and looked up in horror to find Bitsy, the scrambler extraordinary, two courts down the stadium expanse with his racket on the ball! When Bitsy's return failed to win the point, he rolled the entire stadium audience in the aisles by taking off his cap, bowing low and yelling across the length of the stadium, "Baron, you are just too good!"

One final bit of advice to the volleyer—don't goof. When presented with a setup, don't oblige by making a spectacular error. After working hard to force the opponent into hitting up a feeble sitter, it is sort of disconcerting, to say the least, to knock it into the net or out. During the course of a three-set match the experts only goof two or three times. Take your time, watch the ball, don't overhit, and you should be able to reduce drastically the number of goofs.

the Net Strokes

The volley is a short, crisp, punch stroke—like a boxer's jab—requiring little or no backswing and only a short follow-through. The only exception to this is the drive or swinging volley—a flat volley used to impart speed to a high soft return in order to put the ball away.

The net position is 6 to 9 feet from the net, depending on your height and speed of reflexes. The best net stance is a slight forward crouch with feet about two feet apart and weight on the balls of the feet for better agility. The racket is held with head slightly up pointing at the net so you can swing to either side with the same rapidity. The best grip is the continental, as the same grip can be used for forehand, backhand and overhead.

The ball should be struck in front of you with wrist cocked slightly upward and firm as demonstrated by Budge in figures 32 and 33. Your body should be turned sideways to the net when time permits you to step into the ball. If you must play a low volley, bend down to it—do not just drop your racket head (figure 34). Bending the knees and getting down to the ball to maintain your wrist below the racket head is the secret of good volleying (girls, who are the biggest offenders, please take note). You will stroke the ball more effectively partly because your eyes can follow the ball onto the racket with far greater accuracy when down near the level of the ball. The low volleys are defensive since you must hit up with little pace, whereas killers can be scored whenever the ball is above net level.

The volley stroke is made somewhat differently under certain circumstances. If you are forced to stretch to the limit to reach the ball, a flick of the wrist may be required to achieve speed and direction in the return. Low volleys which have to be played well in front of you are usually best played with a slicing motion. And, if you wish to play a drop or stop volley, you must take the punch out of the shot with a loose wrist and little follow-through.

One way to picture the volley stroke is to consider that the racket and stiff wrist present a concave wall, much like a giant dish, from which the opponent's shot will rebound over the net. On low shots the wall is sloped upward, just as is the open racket face. At shoulder height the wall is perpendicular to the ground, just as the racket face is flat at the moment of impact. And above shoulder height the wall slopes inward and downward indicating that the volley should also be struck downward with force.

103

figure 32

Short punch characterizes the backhand volley as well as the forehand. With the racket head held slightly above your locked wrist, the racket travels about 12 to 18 inches as you take a short step into the ball. The angle of the racket head is increased with lower shots.

Like catching baseball, you start the volley with the racket head where the mitt would be. Then, taking a short forward step with the left foot, the arm and racket as one lever make their short, sharp movement into the oncoming ball. The best volleyers are those who confine themselves to the essential motions of the shot and thus minimize the area in which they operate. When hitting a volley above the level of the net cord, snap the wrist; lower volleys must be played with wrist locked.

figure 33

figure 34

Richard A. Gonzales

The perennial professional champion, Big Pancho, demonstrates here the volleying form which has made him famous. As he stretches for the ball, note that his knees are bent so that his firm wrist is below the racket head as he concentrates with every fiber to meet the ball in front of his body.

figure 35

Suzanne Lenglen

*The petite French star shows here the form
which won her many titles, cheers and also
whistles from her male fans. Note the
excellent technique as she strokes the overhead in front of the body with flat racket
face and slightly exaggerated scissor kick
action to reach the height required.*

The overhead is one of ·the most difficult shots in tennis to master,
requiring absolute eye-on-the-ball discipline, as wind and sun can upset the
shot. It is struck by most of the top players with the service (eastern
backhand) grip or the continental grip. A major difference between the
overhead and the serve is the angle of the racket face at moment of impact.
The serve, you will recall, is hit with a stationary ball and the racket is
drawn across the ball to impart a spin. Against a moving ball it is most
difficult to avoid an error by any such tactics. Therefore, the overhead is
properly played by turning the wrist so that the racket meets the ball
with a flat face or with slight slice for control. Direction is imparted by
wrist and arm motion, not spin.

The overhead is similar to the flat serve in almost all particulars: the
ball is hit from the top of the service windup with body turned sideways
to the net until the moment of impact. The ball is struck about a foot
in front of the body, the only difference in stroke production being that
the ball is ordinarily hit down a bit more, and the feet may well be off
the ground in the familiar scissors kick (figure 35). If the lob is
deep and accurate you may be forced to block the ball back deep, rather
than hitting out at an overhead or letting the ball bounce and running
back fast in order that an overhead stroke may be played.

figure 36

William T. Tilden

Every move of Big Bill Tilden on the tennis court was a classic picture of proper form. It is, therefore, particularly fitting to show him demonstrating the difficult half volley. Note the concentration on the ball as it is about to strike the ground, the body at right angles to the net and the wrist locked. The balance is perfect as the body movement is forward toward the net. The follow-through will be short.

Remember that anyone with an adequate serve can have an adequate overhead with a reasonable amount of practice. A major problem with the average player is that the overhead is generally one of the least practiced of all shots.

The backhand overhead is doubtless the shot most often avoided by all classes of players—everyone tries desperately to run around lobs to get them on the forehand side. The reason, of course, is that very few players can hit a backhand overhead with any pace. It is far safer to block such shots back deep or angle them off rather than to try to hit them hard.

The half volley is a shot to be avoided wherever possible, as it is strictly a defensive, difficult-to-control shot used to try to save a situation when you are caught out of position. Only Cochet and Richards among all the greats were rather consistently good at this delicate shot.

The proper method of stroking the half volley is to bend the knees to get down to the ball, take a short back swing with racket face open sufficient to lift the ball over the net and hit firmly through the ball with a short, controlled follow-through (figure 36).

chapter 7

Base
Line
Play

In today's top-flight singles, base line play is the forgotten segment. The long, exciting rallies of the golden era of tennis, as exemplified by the play of Tilden, Johnston, Cochet, Lacoste, Vines, Perry and Budge, are completely missing in the current serve and volley game. While back court still generally prevails on slow composition or clay courts, the only sure way to get to see expert base line exchanges these days is to watch the ranking veterans or ladies. As a result, singles has suffered a real loss in popularity as a spectator sport.

This trend has another disturbing aspect. Since most club or weekend players do not possess the power to play the big game, they learn almost nothing by attending championship tournaments where they can see little other than a serve and a volley each point. Some method of returning the game to the style of "the good old days" would be welcomed by many players and fans. Various things have been tried, such as a three-bounce rule, lengthening of the service line, etc. However, probably the best solution is to standardize international play on one type of slow court.

A clear and comprehensive description of the tactics of base line play is an extremely difficult undertaking. The reason for this is that style of play as well as players themselves vary so much in their effectiveness—those who do well against one type of play may do miserably against another. Only a master like Tilden can cope with any style by choosing to beat his opponent at his own game or by improvising to counter his strengths at every turn. The great tacticians, like Brookes, Lacoste and Riggs, probed until they found weaknesses and then exploited them with precision, skill and determination. Others, like Vines and Helen Wills Moody at their peak, merely blasted the opponent off the court with blistering, deep drives.

Because of the infinite variety of the base line game, it is practical to present only the key points in this chapter. These will·involve sections on forcing shots, passing shots, defensive shots and typical tactical mistakes. Following this will be the all-important section on methods of hitting the ground strokes. But before getting into these in some detail, there are a few over-all tactics to master.

The most important thing to bear in mind is that base line rallies are essentially fencing operations. You must try to "move the opponent around" by one means or another in order to extract an error or a weak return. Moving him around may mean running him from side to side, mixing him up by changing direction, depth, speed or spin, or catching him going in one direction and hitting in the other. Whatever the method, once he hits a bad shot which lands shallow (closer to the net than 10 feet from the base line), you should go for the kill by hitting a forcing shot and moving in to the net. While this is easier to do on a fast court than on a slow one, you must, nevertheless, take advantage of these all-too-rare opportunities whenever the opening is presented. Otherwise the opponent will recover his position and you will have wasted the advantage you worked so hard to gain. For overpowering testimony to the importance of taking advantage of the short ball, remember that data from numerous matches show that seven of eight winners in base line play come as a result of capitalizing on a short ball.

The second thing to remember is to hit within your capabilities. To make errors, however spectacular, leads to naught, but to keep the ball under control and in play leads to victory over many an opponent.

Next, what should now be a familiar requirement, is to work at anticipating each move by your opponent in order that you may cover the wide expanse of court and move into position to make the return. Proper balance and position make this relatively easy, but a move in the wrong direction spells disaster. Between strokes you should ordinarily attempt to return to the basic base line position, which is at the center of the court about a foot behind the base line. In doing so you cannot afford to be leisurely. Concentrate particularly on anticipating the direction and length of your opponent's forehand as it is usually his best stroke. Remember that all those "effortless" players who are always in position really get that way by being tops at anticipation.

And, finally, in striving to improve your base line play, practice keeping the ball deep. This is the trademark of the accomplished player. Your opponent can seldom make a truly offensive return from deep in his court.

Forcing Shots

To become a good singles player you have to develop the ability to hit forcing ground strokes. These are the weapons with which defenses are pierced and openings are gained. As with all strokes in tennis, there are several varieties of forcing shots:

1. *Sheer power type*

   Some players just hit the ball so hard to the corners of the base line that they either run their opponent into the ground, draw weak returns which can be put away or force errors. Examples of typical points by the power players are shown in figures 37 and 38.

2. *Tactical type*

   Most players are not equipped with overwhelming power, so they have to resort in part to cunning. This means being able to outthink or outmaneuver your opponent. Usually this entails a use of change of pace, spin or direction to fool him. Wise tacticians keep forcing shots low to prevent the opponent from lobbing effectively. In fact, on a wet court the smart player takes advantage of the low-bounce conditions and goes to net more often. As in the case of the volley, most forcing shots are hit to the backhand side because the return is usually weaker and lobs can generally be hit on your forehand side. Some typical points are shown in figures 39 and 40.

   Another trick of the tactician is to find a particular weakness of an opponent and then exploit it wisely. This means to exploit it only to gain certain crucial points, as overdoing it may cause him to correct the defect. Since it is not possible to predict all the types of flaws you will encounter in various opponents over the years, we will have to be content here with just trying to emphasize the importance of discovering whatever weakness does exist. Perhaps an example of an actual case involving Davis Cup players will serve this purpose.

We remember vividly a conversation we had one afternoon with a top player as we walked together from the dressing room to the stadium where he had an important match. He confided he thought he had detected a chink in the armor of his opponent (name omitted out of kindness). From watching previous matches he believed that his adversary had a tendency toward errors when forced to run wide and play a ball hit low and deep to his backhand. As our friend took the court we grabbed a seat near the base line and waited anxiously to see what would happen. Any anxiety was short-lived. On the very first point our friend hit a drive deep to his opponent's forehand and then sliced a ball low and deep to the backhand. His opponent, running at top speed, golfed the spinning ball into the bottom of the net. Seeing this, our friend walked quickly back to the spot where we were sitting and whispered with a broad grin, "The match is over." And it was—in three straight sets.

In weekend play weaknesses are more prevalent so that tactical choices can often be broader. If your opponent likes to slug, feed him soft shots and spin. If you hate spin, go to net. If he likes to come to net and you have trouble passing him, beat him to the net position. If he hates to volley, draw him forward. If he cannot run, drop-shot him.

3. *Continuous pressure type*

In a sense, the important business of just getting each ball back as deep as possible is a form of forcing game. This tactic often forces an opponent through plain exasperation. You goad him into becoming more and more impatient, and then he will start to make errors by overhitting the ball or trying shots which are too difficult to make with any consistency. Many a big hitter has been beaten by blowing up under this sort of subtle pressure.

Once the forcing game has created for you the opening represented by a short ball, move in and go for the placement. A good deep or angled drive or slice, or a drop shot from in close should win most points, and a volley of any return will take care of the rest.

figure 37

Classical

These diagrams show the murderous types of forcing shots which should be familiar to all who have watched tournament play.

On the left is shown a sequence which is so deadly the server can often win the point in any of three ways without even bothering to take the net. The server has run the receiver off the court with his serve to the forehand corner and then hit the return deep to the backhand to run him off the court on the other side. When this draws a shallow return, server A has three possible choices for a win. If he notes receiver B is slow in moving back into position, server A can drive the ball beyond his reach to aim point 1. If, on the other hand, receiver B ex-

Forcing Shots

pects this cross-court return and starts running hard to his right, the server can hit behind him deep to aim point 2, or slice one shallow and wide to aim point 3.

On the right is shown the proper method of forcing following a weak return to the middle. The idea is to waste no time once an opportunity is presented. Server A drives deep down the line to the backhand, goes in to net on a line to guard against the expected down-the-line return and finds he has the court wide open for a choice of winning volleys. Depending on when and where the receiver starts to move, he can volley deep to aim point 1, angle volley to aim point 2 or volley behind him to aim points 3 or 4.

figure 37

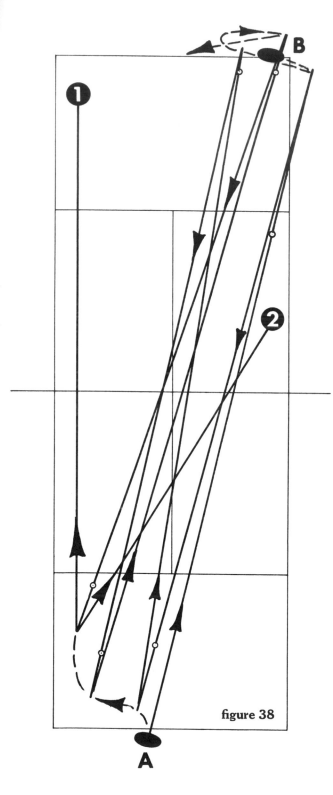

figure 38

Taking Advantage of

Much of forcing base line play is fencing for a shallow return and capitalizing on it.

On the left is shown a classic sequence often used by the great clay court players like Parker. The serve is kept to the backhand corner and a series of backhand exchanges is started. The purpose of the server is to push the receiver further and further to his left until he draws a shallow return. Once this happens he can then crack one down the line to aim point 1. As the players put it, the receiver would need a bicycle to reach this one. If, in fact, he were pedaling fast to try to cover the down-the-line shot, the server can still earn a placement. He does this by faking the drive and then changing direction and hitting a soft sharply-angled shot cross court to aim point 2 to wrong-foot the receiver.

the Shallow Return

On the right is shown another classic maneuver after a very shallow return. In this case the server has proceeded to run the receiver hard with a sequence consisting of a wide serve to the backhand, a slice wide and low to the forehand and a drive deep to the backhand corner. Receiver B has just managed to get the latter back with a weak shot landing in the middle of the service court. As server A approaches the ball, he fakes a hard drive to either corner to keep his opponent deep and then hits a delicate drop shot to aim point 1 or 2. In baseball parlance, the pitchers call this pulling the string. Such tactics are especially good if the court is slow or the opponent is slow or tired. The ladies (slower runners) use this shot against one another with telling effectiveness.

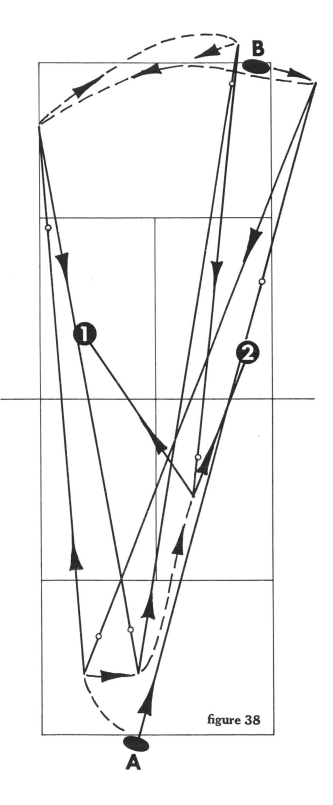

figure 38

119

Passing Shots

To capture a set in tennis you have to be able to break the opponent's service at least once. This means it is an absolute must to have in your arsenal of weapons some effective passing shots if you are to win against the serve and volley demons of today.

Your chances of passing anyone at net depend in large measure on how far you are from the net at the moment you strike the ball. On balls which land within about 10 feet of the base line, your chances of passing a good volleyer are almost nil. But on any ball landing closer in, the odds should shift in your favor. Data taken from many matches serve to emphasize these statements. Successful passing shots are made only one in four tries (omitting errors) from a ball landing within 10 feet of the base line. However, from 10 to 18 feet (the service line) from the base line, two out of three passing shots are winners. And from within the service line, the volleyer is a sitting duck—the passer can beat him seven out of eight times. Before you think this is too easy, just remember you have to be able to anticipate and move in to reach the short volley in time before it can be turned into a passing shot.

Since the passer is presented with a short ball only about one in three times, you cannot afford to miss very often. An important part of not missing is anticipating when to expect a short ball and where it will probably land, so that you can get set for your passing shot. There are several typical opportunities on which you can capitalize, such as:

1. A return of service which forces the net-rushing server to volley up from his feet near the center of the service line is liable to result in a weak return, usually near the center.

2. Any return which forces the volleyer to reach far to one side will usually result in a short volley hit down the line.

3. Any return which the net player must half-volley will ordinarily be lifted with little pace. If you can anticipate the direction, you should have plenty of time to move to the right spot and note the best passing possibilities.

4. Any dink return which the netman must volley up from close to the net will usually result in a short volley hit cross court over the center of the net, since this is the lowest portion of the net.

In connection with passing, do not underestimate the value of the lob. It is not just a desperation shot to be used only when run off the court. On short balls the offensive lob is a powerful tool, especially when the shot is hidden (see figure 41). Masters like Tilden beat top opponents like Borotra using the well-masked lob in preference to other passing shots. And if the opponent is crowding the net or moving in, even a defensive lob is liable to become a winner. The professionals employ the lob extensively and expertly to keep the opponent from playing on top of the net. On a low-bounding ball, deep in the court, it is best to use the very high defensive lob. The young and old tennis player can improve his game greatly by studying the use of the lob as demonstrated by such experts as Gonzales, Rosewall and Hoad. They have perfected the offensive and defensive use of this important weapon and never hesitate to use it. The lob is the most underrated shot in tennis; all players would do well to practice it.

A number of base line and all-court plays to illustrate the infinite variety of tennis and the importance of a courageous defense are shown in figures 41 and 42.

Some typical tactical mistakes are illustrated in figures 43 and 44.

To extricate yourself from the defensive position represented by the base line area takes a combination of patience, skill and determination seasoned with a proper amount of dash, daring and imagination.

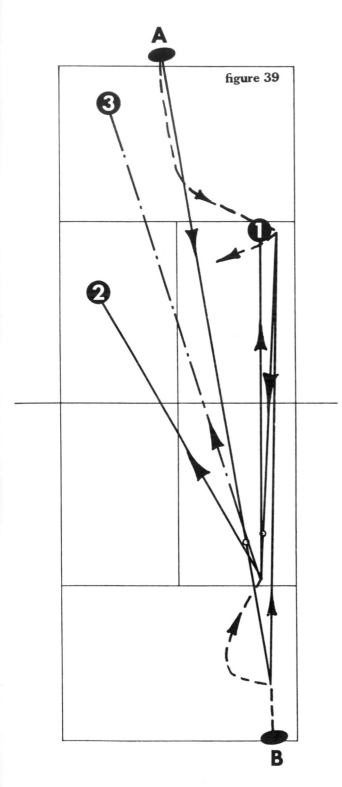

figure 39

Classical Passing

The success of the passer depends on forcing the net-man to volley short—within a few feet of the service line at the maximum. Once you do so, you have to make your passing shot count by placing it carefully, but not trying to raise chalk dust with each shot. In fact, you win more points by drawing an error from the volleyer by making him reach than you do by executing a clean pass. On very short balls it is often best to hit the passing shot right at the chest of the volleyer to draw an error.

On the left is shown a favorite tactic for receivers against net-rushing servers. The serve is somewhat shallow so receiver B moves in and hits the return early and low down the line. This catches server A near the service line and forces him to reach far to his left to make the volley from near the ground. The receiver should anticipate a volley hit up weakly and in a down-the-line direction. There is practically nothing else the server can do. Thus, the receiver should move in a bit and get set to capitalize on the short volley, as shown. He must watch the server as well as the ball. If the server starts to

Shots

move to the center, the passing shot can be chipped safely down the line to aim point 1. And if the server is slow to recover, the receiver has a wide-open court to hit a slightly-topped passing shot cross court — with room to spare — to aim point 2. If the server moves in close to the net to try to cut off either return, an offensive lob can be dumped neatly over his head to aim point 3.

On the right is depicted one of the most common passing situations encountered against the net-rushing server. Here the return of service is a sharply-angled, low cross-court slice or dink which forces the server to volley up. He will usually do so cross court because the net is too high to hit effectively down the line. Sensing this you can get set for the passing shot. This is a thrilling situation as it necessitates outguessing the net player. He knows you will go cross court to aim point 1 if he runs too far to his right, or down the line to aim point 2 if he lingers. Against a good net player you have to note his actions and hide your intentions to the last second. If you do, you have an easy winner, and, if not, he has an easy volley for the point. So be careful!

figure 39

123

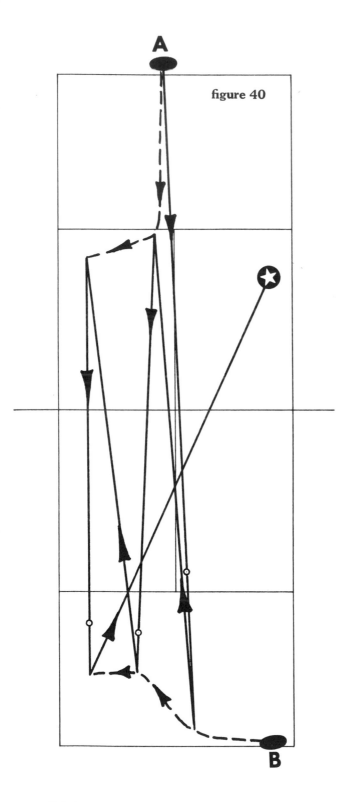

figure 40

Engineering

While outright passing shots which whiz through narrow paths past the net player are beautiful to behold, it is much more likely that success is achieved only after two or more carefully selected shots, the last of which wins or draws an error. This figure shows two examples.

On the left receiver B returns service cross court to a point near the service line. At this moment receiver B should sense the passing possibilities. Since the server is volleying from near the service line, he will probably not be able to play a truly forcing shot. So receiver B properly moves a step inside the baseline, hoping for a short return. When server A obliges, he is ready to move in while observing the moves of the netman. As he sees server A start to cover the middle, he elects to chip low down the line. By this maneuver he forces server A to reach far for the ball and volley up. Since this should result in a weak volley down the line, receiver B gets set for such a return. When this happens he has successfully created the opening he needs. With server A way on the righthand side of the court, B can hit a cross-court passing shot for a well-deserved win. Or, if server A

the Pass

moves too rapidly cross court, the receiver can cross him up by hitting the passing shot behind him down the line.

On the right is shown a point played by Olmedo against Rosewall, with Olmedo engineering a fine passing sequence under the pro three-bounce rule. Olmedo serves to Rosewall's backhand and the point begins with a familiar base line pattern of cross-court returns answered by down-the-line returns. Rosewall decides to take the net on his backhand down the line and Olmedo returns with a soft, low forehand to the middle to try to draw a short volley. Olmedo starts moving a bit forward in expectation, so that it is easy for him to get set for the short return when it occurs. As he sees Rosewall move toward the middle, Olmedo decides to hit a delicate spinning, cross-court backhand dink just over the net. Olmedo properly anticipates that this will force Rosewall to volley up, so once again he moves forward to take advantage of the opportunity. He is rewarded for his excellent tactics by a weak volley which he, in turn, is able to volley away down the line to complete a beautiful exhibition of a passing sequence.

figure 40

125

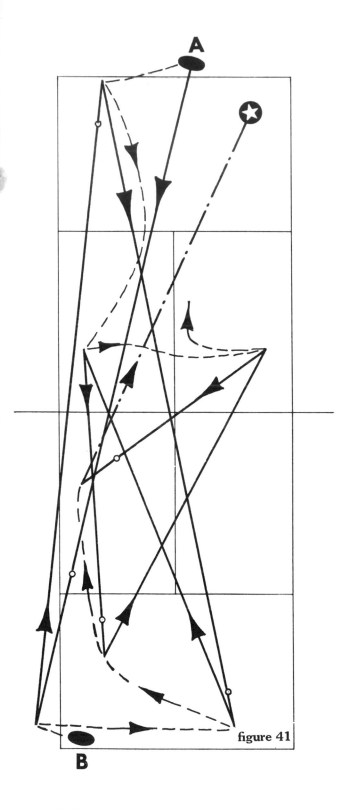

figure 41

Defense and

Here are two points which show the defensive touch of the pros. When in trouble, they set an example for all tennis players in their efforts to extricate themselves.

On the left Rosewall, the receiver, returns serve down the line and is promptly run wide to the forehand as his opponent takes the net. Here Rosewall hits a soft, topped forehand cross court which the opponent has to hit up a bit. This gives Rosewall time to cover the volley. From this point he hits a soft crosscourt backhand dink, which again forces the net player to volley up. At this moment Rosewall anticipates a crosscourt return and moves forward. As a result, he is able to fake down the line and then lob the return beautifully cross court to the corner for a fine point.

Rosewall often crosses his opponent by hitting the unusual shot — a backhand lob down the line.

Scrambling

On the right Sedgman, server A, gets into trouble by making a short first volley. The receiver lobs and Sedgman is just able to get back to block a backhand overhead deep to the corner. The opponent tries to catch him by hitting a cross-court passing shot as Sedgman is going back in to the net. But Sedgman anticipates in time to reverse direction and tries to cross up the opponent by dumping a little drop shot down the line. This is noted by the opponent and he roars in to cover the shot. As he does so, Sedgman is in a desperate position—he must anticipate the direction of the next shot. As he moves to the center, he sees the opponent reach around the ball toward the right side line which signifies a cross-court shot. At this, Sedgman pours on the coal toward the side line and is just able to reach the ball and poke it down the line for a great win.

figure 41

127

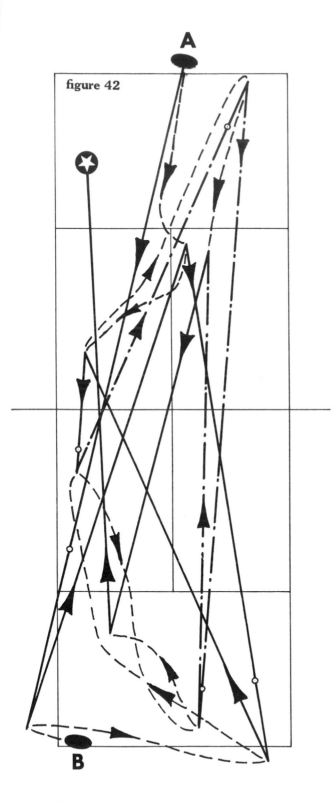

figure 42

Never Give Up

In the tense moments of an important match, the players are keyed up to the point where they will pull off remarkable shots. This means two things: never assume the opponent will miss and never give up trying to retrieve the ball.

On the left is a fabulous point recorded in Davis Cup play. Server A serves wide to the backhand and volleys the return cross court for what would often be a placement. But the receiver is so fast in covering court that he is able to run past the ball and make a topped cross-court return. The server replies by dumping a little drop volley just over the net. Again the agile receiver gets to what might have been another winner and is able to lob deep. The server scrambles back, returns a deep lob and rushes in to the net. The receiver tries to surprise him by hitting back another lob. As he sees the server will, indeed, have to play an off-balance overhead aimed to the backhand side, receiver B elects to take a gamble. He moves forward to cut off the shot

the Ship

and is rewarded by being able to block a volley down the line for a sensational win of a point seemingly lost at least twice!

On the right is shown a point played at the 1958 National Clay Court Championship. Here server A plays a deep cross-court forcing shot off the return of service, and takes the net. Receiver B plays a delicate cross-court dink which forces the server to volley up short cross court. The tide now turns in favor of the receiver as he anticipates well and moves in to hit down the line. But the shot is not quite deep enough and server A is able to reach the ball after a hard run. He plays a high defensive lob which receiver B gets set to put away in routine fashion. But his play is too routine. He fails to hide his direction so that the scrambling server is able to cover the ball and hit a sensational down-the-line passing shot for a win. And no one is more surprised than receiver B, who wrongly assumed the point was over and just stood there watching as though in a trance.

figure 42

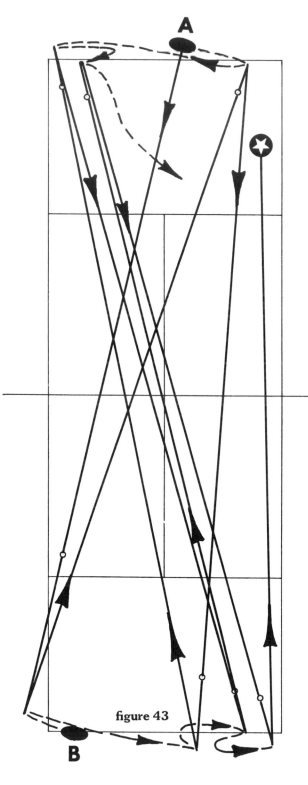

figure 43

Tactical

Even the top players make tactical errors at times. Perhaps it will be refreshing as well as helpful to the week-end player to show a few horrible examples.

The goof on the left was made by one of the top pros— we will, mercifully, omit his name. Here, after the return of service, an exchange of cross-court forehand drives is begun. After the third one, server A decides to take the net on still another cross-court forehand. In so doing he violates three principles— this makes his path to the proper volleying position the longest possible, gives the opponent the widest passing angle and puts the ball on the opponent's strong fore-hand side. As a result, re-ceiver B is able to drive down the line for an easy outright placement which al-

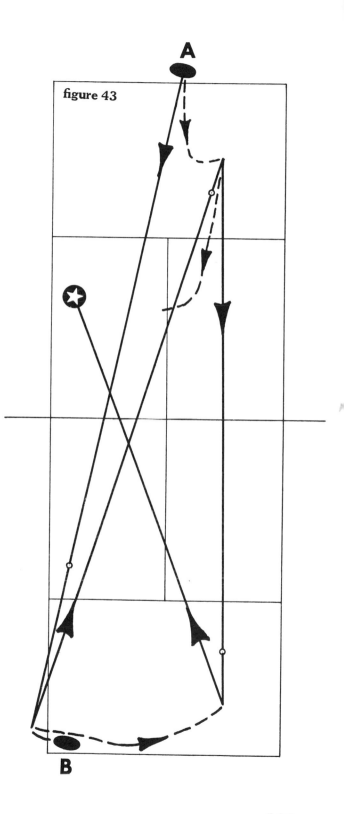

figure 43

Errors

most any weekend player could also have produced.

The bad move on the right is typical in many a match. Receiver B has returned service a bit shallow cross court. So server A smells an easy win and decides to gallop in behind a down-the-line approach shot. But the forcing shot is not forcing at all. Despite the fact that it is too shallow and too near the middle, server A has so made up his mind that he continues his move toward the net. This presents receiver B with a ridiculously easy passing situation. With server A caught back near the service line, it is simple to hit a cross-court shot to the wide-open spaces. Perhaps it should be noted that there is no law against changing your mind about going to net if you hit a poor approach shot.

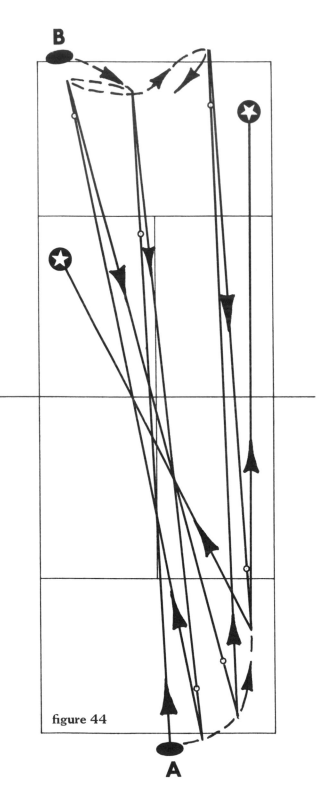

figure 44

More Tactical

Let us continue the lessons on what not to do.

On the left the point starts out well for receiver B. He makes a good, deep return of service and exchanges deep forehand drives. Next server A drives fairly deep down the line. At this juncture receiver B hits just about the worst possible return — shallow back down the line. As will be seen from the diagram, server A has been handed the point on a silver platter. All he has to do is to hit a topped cross-court shot for a winner or wrong-foot the receiver by hitting back down the line.

On the right is depicted

Slips

the misuse of the drop shot. After a semi-deep return, server A tries a drop shot from a short distance inside the base line. Unless the opponent has just broken his leg skiing or has his eyes shut, he will have half the day to cover any drop shot hit from deep in the court. As shown, receiver B has merely to play a sharp cross-court drop shot or a drive down the line to win after such a tactical mistake. Yet this point was actually played at Forest Hills! Incidentally, this also illustrates how easy it is to win a point when playing a ground stroke at net as recorded in Table VI.

figure 44

the Forehand

The anticipatory position (1), your position of security to which you return after every shot. The body, well relaxed, is poised on the toes, weight forward. The racket is cradled in the left hand, ready for the next shot. Start moving from the anticipatory position as soon as you sense the direction of the oncoming ball. Never taking your eye off the ball, pivot on right foot and cross over with the left, keeping body sideways to net (2). Put your entire weight on back foot and counterbalance with left arm. Racket head continues back, reaching top part of arc, face of racket still open (4).

the Ground Strokes

The workhorse of tennis is the forehand drive, the staple of the game for most players. It can be the big stick with which to beat down your opponent or the last bulwark of defense when all else fails.

The forehand and backhand—the so-called ground strokes of tennis—are useful in direct proportion to their pace, depth, accuracy and deception. Pace and depth come only from the perfect blending of those magic ingredients of any good athletic stroke—coordination and timing; or, in simpler terms, the ability to lean your weight and strength into the shot at the exact moment you strike the ball. Accuracy and the ability to place the ball you will learn by subtle shifts in ball-racket angles and in the distribution of your weight. The weight is about evenly divided between the two feet on shots down the right side line; on cross-courts shots it is shifted to the left foot somewhat sooner. Deception is accomplished by always beginning the stroke the same way and setting the direction and spin or lack of spin at the last moment in the execution of the shot.

Two important pointers on ground strokes: bend the knees so that you get down to the ball and never neglect the follow-through—always finish the shot.

For purposes of initial illustration of the classical eastern forehand drive we have selected the simple, fluid, effortless sweep of Budge as shown in figure 45.

Among the other great forehands were those of Johnston, Vines, Perry and Kramer.

figure 45

the Forehand
(continued)

Elbow and arm straighten as the racket head travels below ball and weight transfers to left foot. Left arm leads forward thrust (5). Note fluid body motion. Finish of shot finds the racket head slightly above shoulder level to give free and confident follow-through (8). The weight remains forward as arm and racket action pull right side around to anticipatory position and the left hand resumes its hold on racket. Firm wrist propels racket forward, full body weight leaning in, racket head below wrist, elbow away from body (6). With arm fully extended, hit the ball comfortably about 18 inches in front of the left foot (7). The eyes must always be fixed on ball.

On the forehand, each arm should describe a perfect arc in the course of the stroke. The left arm follows the right arm into the hitting position and starts the racket head on its backward motion before turning the work load over to the right. As the right arm takes over, it completes the backswing with the racket head high. Then the right shoulder drops, guiding the racket into the bottom of the arc just before it meets the ball. As contact is made, the full force of the racket is brought against the lower inside of the ball. The wrist is cocked until point of contact, when it locks with the forearm to utilize full power. The left arm swings forward and around in front of the body to aid in balance. The stroke is always completed with a full follow-through.

figure 45

figure 46

3

2

1

the Backhand

Anticipatory position (1) is facing net, on your toes for quick movement, with racket held easily in both hands, elbows in close. Then pivot on left foot (2) as left arm pulls racket and torso back. Body pivot (3) comes next, stepping over with right foot so back is half turned to net. Right hand makes a quarter turn to left for grip change and receives work load as racket head reaches highest point of arc (4).

The backhand drive is executed on the same mechanical principle as the forehand drive. Properly hit, it can be just as effective as the forehand. The average player finds the backhand shot more difficult than the forehand, but actually it should be easier because you're swinging away from your body. Contrary to general belief, it should be an attacking and not a defensive weapon.

To illustrate the backhand we have selected the great stroke of Budge, the strongest in his repertoire, and a stroke without an ounce of lost motion (figure 46). Note especially his perfect weight distribution—from left to right—and his free and easy follow-through. A good rule is to get as close to your work as possible without cramping, so as to meet the ball comfortably in the center of the racket head. You should never be so far from the ball as to feel you have to make an undue effort to reach it. Note also how the elbow, as in the forehand stroke, is held close to the body until forward motion starts—then straightens to release coiled energy.

5

6

the Backhand

(continued)

Racket head drops into position (5) and starts below flight of the ball, right shoulder well down (6). Right arm is straightened, brought around body. Hit into and straight through (7), transferring weight from left leg to right. Naturally following through, racket ends at shoulder level or slightly higher (8). Body remains collected yet relaxed, leaning into the stroke. Left arm counterbalances and permits a full and easy follow-through motion (7 and 8). The last step is a pivot on the right foot (9) to bring feet, knees, hips, shoulders, head, eyes, arms and racket back to anticipatory position (1). The circle of action is then complete.

7

8

9

figure 46

figure 47

Baseball swing is the analogy used by Budge to describe backhand motion. He has likened it to the swing of Ted Williams.

The left arm is unusually important to a good backhand. To start with, it does most of the work in taking the racket back to the start-forward position. From this point it serves an equally vital function in helping achieve and maintain balance. An interesting and sound formula to follow is that of executing a perfect circle in preparing for and completing the shot. Wait for the shot from the squared position (always on your toes), pivot, swing, follow-through and return to the original position, waiting for the next shot (figures 48 and 49).

The backhand must be a fluid and continuous motion, not a series of separate acts performed one after the other. Properly executed, the steps are simple and related, creating a natural sequence without hesitation or acceleration. Starting with the anticipatory position in the backcourt, the right hand is relaxed on the handle, the throat of the racket cradled lightly in the left. As the ball approaches, you move into position, following the flight of the ball. That is of the utmost importance. The left hand guides the racket until the downward arc begins, when the right hand tightens its grip. At point of contact—approximately 12 inches in front of the right foot—the ball should be met waist high. If the bounce is low the knees should be bent more to meet the ball at its height. The shot should be made with a firm grip, the wrist straightening and locking naturally at the time of contact.

The forehand lob starts with the motions of the forehand drive and then the action changes at the last moment to an upward motion with a shorter than normal follow-through. The offensive lob should be a surprise shot, so that it is vital to hide your intentions by employing your usual backswing. The best lobbers also roll the wrist a bit to put a top on the low, offensive lob in order to make the ball drop faster and bound away from the retriever.

The backhand lob should be hit just as the forehand, except that it is almost always hit with underspin with an open racket face.

Both offensive and defensive lobs should be aimed as near the base line as possible. The defensive lob is usually hit higher than the offensive lob to give one a greater margin of error and to allow time to get back into position. Actually the lob is an excellent shot which most young players would do well to utilize more often. An offensive lob to the backhand is difficult for any net player to handle. An even the high, deep defensive lob is not easy to hit with an overhead, particularly if the wind and sun are playing tricks. Often the only safe play the netman has is to permit the ball to bounce and then hit a service stroke overhead.

The drop shot is hit like a chop but with a short follow-through. The shot is a delicate one requiring great touch. The ball should be hit clearing the net with plenty to spare, yet bounce within about 8 feet of the net, and have so much backspin on it that it does not bound toward the retriever, but falls dead. It takes plenty of practice to be able to employ this tricky shot with confidence.

The chop has gone out of style as a basic ground stroke, as it floats enough to give an advantage to an opponent at net. It is murder, however, against a baseliner on a wet grass court with its skidding bounce. The chip, dink and slice can be used from the base line, just as on return of service, to force the net player to volley up unless he is on top of the net, in which case you resort to the lob.

In the popular rush to the serve and volley big game many of the younger players have neglected the development of their ground strokes. This is responsible more than any one thing for the clamor in some quarters to change various rules in order to put more rallies back into tennis. Others, like Budge, claim there is absolutely nothing wrong with tennis that some good ground strokes won't fix.

figure 48

Maureen Connolly

That the girls can also blast backhand drives is beautifully illustrated here by "Little Mo" Connolly. Noted for her powerful ground strokes and great foot work, she shows here the reason why. Using the classical eastern backhand grip, she demonstrates a perfect high follow-through with knees bent and foot action indicating she is already starting to move back into position in the middle of the base line.

figure 49

Alice Marble

Many top players use a backhand drive which starts with the racket head high on the backswing and then slices under the ball with racket face open on the follow-through. Here one of the best ladies of all time shows perfectly how to bend the knees, get down to the ball and drive it down the line with speed and accuracy.

chapter 8

Summary

The game of singles in tennis is more than an athletic contest of strength, stamina, agility and skill—it is also an intellectual contest. There is a defense for every attack and an attack for every defense, and often the more intelligent and adroit player can overcome the "stronger" player. This is because he develops tactical plans based on his own strengths and his opponent's weaknesses in order to force the opponent to accept battle under the least favorable conditions at every possible opportunity.

When one adds the intricacies of stroke production to the extensive tactical variations of tennis, there is little wonder that mastery of all of the secrets of the game becomes a very long and difficult task. But it is equally true that a real knowledge of a number of fundamentals of each will go a long way toward making a tennis player. Once these are clearly understood and kept continually in mind, the player can then concentrate on the finer points, such as depth and anticipation, which ultimately spell excellence. It is the purpose of this book to try to present the fundamentals in a manner to provide a useful and sound foundation for beginner and expert alike.

To begin this summary at the beginning, let us first review briefly the basic principles of stroke production.

Perhaps the single most important thing to remember is that all the great champions of past and present have had one thing in common: they made the game look ridiculously easy. While their style and grips and methods of meeting the ball varied in certain details, they all developed simple, fluid strokes which were a delight to behold. Every move was made with perfect footwork and balance and no stroke was cluttered with unnecessary motions.

This is the direction in which the aspiring player must move. To be sure, you can learn tennis up to a point by following the methods of the great. You can start by adopting the eastern grip and the basic backswing, follow-through, weight shift and footwork of the champions until you can enjoy the game by keeping the ball in play with consistency. It is particularly important to get down to the ball (bend the knees) on ground strokes and volleys, keep your eye on the ball as you stroke it and to practice your toss to achieve a forcing serve. From this point on you have to develop your own style in detail depending on the particular physical equipment you possess. Obviously, a Cochet cannot hit shots in the same manner as a Budge. And despite the similarity in physique of Budge, Kramer and Gonzales, you can recognize them on a tennis court a mile away by their differences in style. In developing your own game do not overlook the assistance of experienced coaches and professionals. It is usually far easier for such persons to spot flaws in your methods than for you to discover them yourself.

The serve is the single most important stroke in modern offensive tennis. A strong serve is a must—it puts the striker on the offensive, and should of itself open the door for wins in a staggering 40 per cent of points by forcing weak returns of service or errors. The big serve is twice as effective on fast courts as on slow clay or composition courts.

The primary things to remember are to get the first serve in and to keep all serves deep. The experts accomplish both some 80 per cent of the time. The real hallmark of a top server is a player who can keep his second serve deep. Good first serves and good deep deliveries, whether first or second serves, ultimately produce a won point in about 75 per cent of the cases.

On fast courts the top players follow every serve rapidly to the net and attempt to volley any return away for a winner. First serves are usually aimed toward the side lines to open up the court, and second serves at the backhand corner. On slow courts the server usually hits for the backhand corner and only occasionally follows serve in to the net position since returns of service are more effective on such surfaces.

To win in tennis you have to be able to break the opponent's service. In order to blunt his most important weapons, it is essential to develop a good return of service—one of the most difficult as well as important shots in the game. This you can do only if you pay attention to details. Receiving position is important—a foot or more inside the base line on a line bisecting the possible angle of service delivery is recommended. To be able to get your racket on the speeding ball, you must also work on anticipation of the type and direction of serve the opponent is about to hit. By far the most important thing, of course, is to get the ball back—if you don't, you have lost the point, and if you do, you have an almost even chance of ultimately winning. If you can control the ball, as well as get it back, you should try to hit it low against a net-rushing server to force him to volley up, and deep to the base line against a server who stays back in order to keep him pinned back. The delight of all receivers is the "fat" serve that lands shallow in the service court. Such serves should be eaten alive by moving in and pounding them down the line or, occasionally, sharply cross court. Avoid returns to the center of the court, as they are easiest for the server to handle. Returns to the side lines should win 50 to 60 per cent of the time, whereas returns to the middle will give the volleyer a 70 to 80 per cent chance of winning. Whenever possible, the receiver should try to grab the offensive by taking the net. A determined receiver, equipped with nerve, audacity, good ground strokes and the ability to mix up the direction, speed and spin of his returns, can drive the server crazy by forcing him to work to the limit for every point.

Attack is the foundation of modern tennis. The percentages favor the attacker, and tennis is a percentage game. The net position is the best location from which to exploit the attack, as shown by the fact that net play accounts for close to one third of all points won. No longer can any player think of the volley and overhead as strokes reserved for the experts. Rather, these strokes represent the easiest possible way of finishing off a point once you have forced the opponent out of position. Volleying his return sharply gives the opponent no time to recover, whereas waiting on the base line for the ball affords him plenty of time to amble back into position, as well as to glance around at all the beautiful girls in the gallery during the process. The clincher is that volleying is also superb fun.

The best volleyers prepare the path to the net properly by hitting a forcing approach shot to draw a weak, easy-to-volley return. Poor approach shots make the volleyer extremely vulnerable. The volley should really be thought of as a combination of a forcing approach shot followed by a volley. The most important things to remember are to keep the aproach shots deep and, when you take the net, to move in close (within 6 to 9 feet) so you can volley down severely or angle the ball sharply. Always assume each volley will be returned and, as you anticipate the speed and direction, shift your volley position accordingly.

The toughest volley to make is the first volley because it is stroked as you run in and must often be hit up from your shoe-tops, or hit when you are scrambling and reaching to the limit. Unless presented with an easy placement opportunity, the best tactic by far is to hit the first volley deep (within 8 to 10 feet of the base line). Few players can pass you from deep in the court, especially from the backhand side. In fact, the chances of winning the point after a deep first volley are about nine to one in your favor. If, on the other hand, you hit a shallow volley to the danger area in the middle of the court, disaster results—you will be passed or forced to err about six or seven out of ten times.

When both players are on the base line, there is one overriding rule—keep the ball deep. The whole base line game consists of fencing until you can force the opponent into hitting a ball short. This provides you the opportunity of moving in and hitting a forcing shot, deep or angled, which you can turn into a winning point. (It is too risky to try to get in to the net from deep in the court.) Actually about seven out of eight base line points are won after one of the players hits a short shot. The other player can then take advantage of this opening in two ways. In about two out of three cases he can win the point with a forcing shot which will score a placement, or elicit an error. In the third case he can make his forcing shot, follow it in to the net and then volley away the return for the point. During base line rallies assume each shot will be returned and concentrate on anticipating its direction and depth so that you can move to the proper position.

Earlier we mentioned the need for the net player to volley the ball deep until he has an opening for a placement. If we consider this now from the standpoint of the defender, the importance of taking advantage of any short volleys will become evident. When the volley is within 10 feet of the base line, it is very difficult to pass the net player. About the best you can do is to try to force him to volley up or, if he is on top of the net, to lob. Even so you will win only about one out of four or five times. But if the volley lands between the service line and a point 10 feet from the base line, the tide should turn in your favor, provided you hit accurately while masking the direction of your shot. And, if the volley lands within the service court, you should be able to pass the net player over 80 per cent of the time on any ball you can reach. The short volley is obviously the true friend of the defender. Whenever you force the net player to hit a shallow volley, be prepared to take unerring advantage of the gift.

If required to pick the one most important factor in winning singles, we would unhesitatingly select that of keeping the ball in play. Errors are the killers in tennis. To emphasize this, let us look at the terrific erosion they produce:

Twenty-five per cent of returns of service are errors. If the receiver can just return the serve, he has an almost even chance to win the point.

Twenty-five per cent of first volleys are errors. If the volleyer can just
    make his first volley, he will find only 50 per cent of his shots are returned.
If the receiver can just return service and return the first volley, he
    has a better than even chance of winning the point.

This explains why the steady player and the great getters are so hard
to beat in singles.

To date all scoring information in tennis mentions only two types of
errors—nets and outs. Actually we think it is more proper to say there
are three kinds of errors—nets, outs and forced errors. In making this
distinction we are following the system used in baseball, where a sufficiently difficult chance is not charged as an error against the fielder, but is
scored as a hit for the batter. When this is done in tennis, it provides a
better picture of the actual play and the value of the forcing game. In
normal scoring, you find that almost 60 per cent of points are won on
errors and 40 per cent are earned through placements or service aces.
The errors are almost equally divided between nets and outs. However,
if you also consider forced errors in scoring you find the reverse is true—
only 40 per cent of points are won by errors, while an overwhelming 60
per cent are won by earned points including forced errors. There is little
doubt the forcing game is king.

Condition and fight are necessary ingredients for a well-rounded tennis
game. Often they determine the outcome, especially in the final set of a
long match. When you are tired you tend to lose concentration—improper
selection of shots increases and errors start to pour off your racket. This
is when courage is needed to fight your way back into the game. The
determination not to lose is, more than any one thing, what made players
like Schroeder great. And anyone who ever watched Gonzales could not
help but notice how he cranks in that extra effort to lift his game whenever
he gets behind.

There are tricks to both conditioning and fighting. Of course the international player must do roadwork; practice starting fast and running backward as well as forward, moving sideways and making quick changes of
direction; eat properly and get sufficient sleep. But even the weekend
player can benefit from the less strenuous tricks of the trade—such things
as wearing comfortable clothes; preventing tired feet through wearing a
pair of cotton socks under his sweat socks; taking deep breaths when
tired and refraining from drinking much during the course of the match.

We say this despite the fact that Dr. James Dwight, the father of American lawn tennis, recommended a spot of brandy in your water when tired! And when you are barely able to drag yourself around the court, there are ways of reviving yourself. One of the best ways we know of to renew the spirit is the method used by one of the greatest fighters in tennis history. When most downtrodden he revitalized himself by making an extra effort to put a decided spring in his walk and to concentrate on watching the ball. The combination of this spirited effort not only revived him, but, at the same time, served to throw consternation into the mind and the game of his opponent. Small tricks of this type can be magical in their effect. When tired, remember to think!

Practice is essential to progress. Some, like Vinnie Richards, began at a tender age by banging a ball against a backboard by the hour. At any tournament you will see the young aspirants practicing ground strokes, volleys and serves until dark, or as long as the officials will let them use the courts. A bit more practice, especially in the art of anticipation, would help most weekend players. The tournament players use practice to correct weaknesses in their games, not to try to win. And if anyone thinks he practices a lot, just remember that Lacoste used to work out for as many as five sets on the morning of an important match!

Next to practice, the best way to sharpen your game is to play in tournaments. The experience of playing under pressure against various opponents adds the all-important ingredient of seasoning. Butterflies flutter in the stomachs of the best before a match. There is a bit of psychology even in walking on the court—dapper Fred Perry always looked and acted like a sure winner before he ever hit a ball. To be a good tournament player you have to develop the ability to avoid becoming upset by any distractions from the crowd or your opponent, or by decisions you think to be bad. If off form, often a grin at yourself will relax the tension.

The importance of true sportsmanship in bringing real enjoyment to the game of tennis can hardly be overemphasized. This entails not only devotion to such things as fair play and proper court manners, but also providing assistance to other players and to your local tennis association. Finally, it means going out of your way to thank those who also serve, but without glory—the umpire, linesmen, ball boys and tournament officials.

In parting, we wish you the best of luck in your singles play—may all your tactics please the best of the critics and may all your bounces be true!